Theology Today
6 The Theology of Evolution

Theology Today

GENERAL EDITOR:
EDWARD YARNOLD, S.J.

No. 6

The Theology of Evolution

BY

ERVIN NEMESSZEGHY, S.J.
AND JOHN RUSSELL, S.J.

Nihil Obstat
Jeremiah J. O'Sullivan, D.D.
Censor deputatus
29 August 1972

Imprimatur
Cornelius Ep. Corcag. & Ross
2 September 1972

SBN 85342 291 5

ACKNOWLEDGEMENTS

The Scripture quotations in this publication, unless there is indication to the contrary, are taken from the Revised Standard Version of the Bible, copyrighted 1946 and 1952 by the Division of Christian Education of the National Council of Churches of Christ in the U.S.A. and used by kind permission. The quotations from *The Documents of Vatican II* (ed. W. M. Abbott S.J.) are printed by kind permission of the America Press and Geoffrey Chapman, London. The English translation of the passages from *H. Denzinger & A. Schönmetzer, Enchiridion Symbolorum, Definitionum et Declarationum* is adapted from *The Teaching of the Catholic Church* (ed. K. Rahner S.J.) and used by kind permission of The Mercier Press. Some parts of the following articles by J. Russell, S.J. are incorporated in this book and used by kind permission of the Editors: *The Theory of Evolution*, The Month, Jan 1956; *Darwin's Early Critics*, The Month, Feb 1960; *Teilhard De Chardin, The Phenomenon of Man* I & II, The Heythrop Journal, Oct 1960 and Jan 1961; *Evolution and Theology*, The Tablet, 16 Sept 1967.

We wish to thank Miss W. Taylor, B.A. for typing the manuscript.

ABBREVIATIONS

Dz   H. Denzinger & A. Schönmetzer,
Enchiridion Symbolorum, Definitionum et Declarationum (33rd Edit., Barcelona etc., 1965).

BAC Biblioteca de Autores Cristianos, Madrid.

CONTENTS

PREFACE

There cannot be many Christians left who regard the theory of evolution as a subversive attack on the Christian faith. On the contrary, for several decades theologians have assimilated the theory into their theological thought, and in this way have been able to reinterpret some of the Christian doctrines in suggestive and exciting ways. Such is the aim of this book.

It begins with a brief summary of Christian reactions to Darwin's *Origin of Species,* and a simple and precise account of the present state of scientific opinion. Next the authors treat the theological implications of the theory, in particular with regard to the veracity of the biblical accounts of creation, and the doctrines of original sin and the special creation of the human soul. A last chapter on Teilhard de Chardin, the most influential of theologians of evolution, forms a fitting synthesis and development of the ideas contained in the book.

The authoritative scientific information and full ecclesiastical documentation it contains should make this a book of considerable value, such as could only be written by authors who are notable scientists as well as theologians.

E. J. Yarnold.

INTRODUCTION

When in 1859, after more than twenty years of patient scientific investigation, Charles Darwin published *The Origin of Species*, his book was immediately attacked as contrary to the Christian doctrine of creation. Samuel Wilberforce, a well-known contemporary Anglican bishop, wrote in the *Quarterly Review* that if Darwin's thesis is true, then 'Genesis is a lie, the whole framework of the book of life falls to pieces, and the revelation of God to man as we Christians know it, is a delusion and a snare'. But in spite of the bitter and long debate which followed the publication of Darwin's *Origin of Species* and of his other controversial book *The Descent of Man* (1871), the theory of evolution has gained almost universal acceptance first by scientists and then by theologians. This, however, did not lead to the collapse of the credibility of the Bible, nor did it mean that Christian revelation is a delusion; it led only to a change in our understanding both of the world and the Bible. The aim of this essay is to outline this change and to pin-point some important theological implications of the theory of evolution.

In this introductory chapter a few words must be said about the relation between science and theology. There are two popular views in this matter, both of them inaccurate and erroneous. The first may be characterized by the conviction that there is a head-on clash between science and theology in that they provide rival hypotheses for the understanding of the world we live in; science offers natural, theology supernatural explanations; science is based on observable facts and the rational grasp of these facts, theology on the God-hypothesis, on the mystery of the unknown; as science advances, theology retreats: God is edged out more and more from the universe.

This head-on clash view is still probably prevalent today but in more sophisticated circles another popular opinion can be found, which goes to the other extreme in overemphasizing the difference between science and theology. According to this opinion scientific and theological assertions are so radically different not only in their subject-matter but also in their methods and presuppositions that there can be no interference between them: theological assertions are compatible with any scientific theory, and no scientific theory can have theological implications. In fact the matter is not as simple as that. One may of course agree that the aims and methods of scientific discourse are different from those of theological discourse; nevertheless there is a subtle *indirect* influence of each on the other. Certain scientific theories may stimulate or hinder theological investigation, and the converse of this statement seems to be also true: certain theological doctrines may be helpful or, alternatively, hostile for scientific investigation. If, for example, the cause of a natural disaster or epidemic is thought to be a supernatural agency or the immorality of those whom the epidemic strikes, then these assumptions may well inhibit the scientific investigation of the disease in question. Or, if the theory of evolution is believed to be contrary to the Bible, then it is quite likely that in the case of those who take the Bible as the word of God, their belief will prejudice the assessment of evidence which supports the theory of evolution. History shows quite a number of incidents when scientific theories which later proved to be correct were first opposed by the officials of the Church on theological grounds.

Instead of denying such regrettable incidents we should try to understand the reasons why they could have happened. Undoubtedly one of the main reasons is this: religious beliefs do not exist in isolation from other beliefs about the world and ourselves. Religious beliefs are organised and brought into harmony with the current world-view, and since the latter is changing all the time through scientific progress, it is inevitable that again and again believers feel a tension between science and their religious beliefs spelled out by theology. Yet the tension is not between scientific truths and religious truths as such, but between the new world-picture and the old one in which the religious beliefs are spelled out. New scientific theories may help the reinterpretation of certain theological doctrines and can bring about a deeper understanding of them.

But the advantageous influence between science and theology is not a one-way traffic. Certain theological doctrines may stimulate scientific research. It has been argued by several scientists and theologians that the Christian doctrine of creation played a great part in forming a cultural atmosphere in which science could arise. It is undeniable that science, as we know it, came into existence in Western Europe around the seventeenth century, in a civilization which was notably Christian. It is implicit in the biblical notion of creation that the world was made by God, hence it is good, orderly, apprehensible to human knowledge, and man as a crown of creation is commissioned by God to conquer it. 'Be fruitful and multiply, and fill the earth and subdue it; and have dominion over the fish of the sea and over the birds of the air and over every living thing that moves upon the earth' (Gen 1.28).

The claim that the Christian doctrine of creation may have encouraged man to investigate the world does not, of course, mean that non-Christians cannot be excellent scientists or that a non-Christian civilization is necessarily disadvantageous to scientific activity. Nor need we believe that science as such will eventually lead us to the door of religion, and in particular to Christian religion. Christianity as a creative force in the formation of civilization needs science more than science needs Christianity. But whatever we may think about the complex and indirect interrelation between science and Christian theology, and in particular the theory of evolution and the Christian doctrine of creation, we believe that as far as possible the relative autonomy of each discipline must be maintained. That is why first we examine 'evolution' as a scientific theory, then consider what problems it raises for theology, and finally investigate some of its implications in regard to the problems of Original Sin and that of the 'special creation of the soul'. The last chapter gives a short exposition of the evolutionary vision of Teilhard de Chardin.

CHAPTER 1

EVOLUTION AS A SCIENTIFIC THEORY

The 'Theory of Evolution' is generally understood to mean the theory that all living organisms are descended from one, or a very few, original forms, which are themselves presumed to have arisen ultimately from non-living matter. The theory had been proposed in one form or another before Charles Darwin's time, notably by Buffon (1707-1788), Erasmus Darwin (1751-1802) and Lamarck (1744-1829), but it was Charles Darwin (1809-1882) who was first able to propose the theory in a cogent way with an enormous amount of supporting evidence. His theory, in its time, has been attacked and defended with a degree of violence and prejudice which has made it very difficult for the ordinary onlooker to come to any reliable conclusion. It may therefore be worth while to try to give a brief account of the kind of evidence on which the theory is based. It must be understood, however, that much of the evidence is highly technical, so that its import cannot be adequately conveyed in non-technical terms. We shall attempt no more than a broad outline which may bring out a few of the more salient aspects of the problem.

Biological Classification

It will be necessary to start with some general remarks on the Species: *Canis familiaris*. The species is included in the gins with an individual organism – say Fido, our dog. He belongs to a particular race or variety (e.g. fox-terrier) of the Species: *Canis familiaris*. The species is included in the Genus: *Canis,* together with several other species such as the wolf *(Canis lupus)*, and the jackal. The genus is included in a Family: the *Canidae,* together with other genera such as *Vulpes* (the fox). The family belongs to an Order: *Carnivora,* together with a number of other families, such as *Felidae* (cats), *Ursidae* (bears), etc. The Carnivora, together with some thirty Orders (some of them extinct), are included in the Class: *Mammalia.* The mammals, birds, reptiles, amphibia and fishes are Classes belonging to the Sub-Phylum: *Vertebrata* of the Phylum: *Chordata.* Lastly, the Chordate phylum, together with about sixteen others (Arthropods, Echinoderms, Mollusca etc.) constitute the Animal Kingdom. Plants are classified on similar lines.

Micro- and Macro-Evolution

The evidence for Evolution can be considered under two different aspects: firstly, the small-scale evolution of one species or one genus into another; secondly, large-scale evolution linking up one family with another, one order with another, and so on. These are frequently referred to as micro- and macro-evolution respectively. The evidence for micro-evolution is very strong, and in many cases is virtually conclusive. It comes from the study both of fossils and of living organisms, but the former is perhaps the more striking. In suitable geological formations, where sediments have been laid down uniformly over long periods of time, it is sometimes possible to follow a particular type of organism, such as a sea urchin or an oyster, through a continuous series of changes from an initial to a final form which are undoubtedly different species. Similarly, with relatively minor discontinuities, one genus can often be linked up with another, e.g. among the fossil horses and titanotheres.

It is more difficult to establish the fact that evolution is still proceeding, since even a small evolutionary change requires a time which is long compared with a human lifetime. The evidence is mostly indirect and is not easy to summarise, since it is based upon a multitude of complex genetical data, but some indication of its general nature can be given. The most important evidence is undoubtedly the well-established fact that when a given species exists as a series of isolated communities, with no exchange of population between one and another, the different groups will, almost invariably, tend to diverge from one another, and to become distinct races or sub-species. Almost certainly, if the isolation is maintained for a sufficient time, these develop into distinct species or even genera. A typical example is to be found in the freshwater lakes of Scandinavia. These came into existence at the end of the Ice-Age, about 20,000 years ago, with the melting of the ice which had previously covered the whole land surface. They were colonised by what was presumably a single species of char – a fish which normally lives in the Arctic Ocean and comes up the rivers to spawn. With the retreat of the ice the colonies became isolated from each other and from the sea. In consequence, each lake now has its own variety of char, which are classified into several species and numerous sub-species. Unless we are to suppose that each lake had a distinct variety specially created for it, we can hardly escape the conclusion that a measurable amount of evolution has occurred during the last few thousand years. Many similar examples could be quoted from other parts of the world.

Difficulties of the Notion of a 'Biological Species'

The older arguments against the possibility of evolution were often based upon an incorrect notion of what is meant by a biological species. It has been supposed, for instance, that a species is always a perfectly definite, clearly circumscribed group, and that members of one species can never produce fertile hybrids when crossed with members of another. If these two propositions were universally true, then it would admittedly be difficult to see how evolution could ever transcend the limits of the species. In practice, most species can be clearly defined, and most hybrids between species are infertile, but there are sufficient exceptions to make it clear that no universal law can be laid down on the subject. There are, in the first place, two possible ways of defining a species, which do not always coincide with one another. The first is taxonomic; that is to say, it is based upon systematic differences in the form and structure of organisms. The second is ecological: a species is a group of organisms capable of living a full communal life together and freely inter-breeding. It is well-known that taxonomic classifications are frequently arbitrary; there are certain groups which are regarded by some experts as constituting a single species, and are divided by others into several. The ecological definition is superior when it can be used, since it considers the group as a living community, not simply as dead specimens on a dissecting table. Nevertheless, it also breaks down on occasion. For instance, the Herring Gull and the Lesser Black-Backed Gull occur together in Great Britain but do not inter-breed, yet in other parts of the Northern Hemisphere they are linked together by an almost continuous series of intermediate types. There are two 'species' of Whirligig beetle – *Gyrinus natator* and *Gyrinus substriatus* – which in England will freely hybridise where their ranges overlap, but on the Continent will not. In Scotland the female capercailie will pair with the male blackcock or pheasant if no male of its own species is available, but not otherwise. In the first two of these examples we seem to be faced with a species which is on the point of dividing into two, but has not yet completed the process.

We cannot avoid the difficulties by defining a species as a group whose members, when they interbreed, produce fertile offspring. Hybrids between recognised species may be completely fertile or they may have any degree of reduced fertility down to complete sterility, depending on the species concerned and, sometimes, on other factors as well. Complete sterility is the most usual, but by no means the invariable result. Among plants it is sometimes possible, by using special methods of treatment, to produce completely fertile hybrids not only between different species but even between different genera, as for instance between wheat and rye, radish and cabbage, sugar-cane and bamboo. The products are in each case genuinely new species both in their morphological characters and in the fact that they will not normally hybridise with either parent. In certain cases new species of this sort are known to have occurred naturally: the Spartina grass which for more than fifty years has been spreading around the southern and eastern coasts of this country was the result of a natural cross between two other species of the same genus, which came into contact with each other for the first time on the Hampshire coast towards the end of the nineteenth century.

The Evidence for Micro- and Macro-Evolution

The evidence which has already been discussed, and much more of the same sort which has not been mentioned, makes it virtually certain that micro-evolution has occurred in the past and is still occurring. Although its operation can only be positively identified in relatively few cases, there is no difficulty in supposing that it has operated universally in producing new species and genera within the limits of each family. The occurrence of macro-evolution is less easily established. Partly this is due to the slowness of the process, which makes it impossible to obtain any direct contemporary evidence of its workings. If the evolution of one species into another is to be measured in tens or even hundreds of thousands of years, the evolution of one family into another can hardly be expected to reveal itself within the span of human history. There is, however, a more serious difficulty arising from the unsatisfactory nature of the geological evidence. Although it is frequently possible to link up different species or genera by means of a series of intermediate fossil forms, this is not so with the wider groupings. In no case is it possible to find a reasonably continuous series of transitional forms linking one order with another, and the same is true to a large extent of the families within one order. *A fortiori* it is true also of the classes and the phyla. This fact has been used by critics of evolution as strong evidence against the theory and it does undoubtedly constitute a difficulty which has not been fully resolved. It is not, however, quite so damaging as it might appear at first sight. For many reasons, gaps in the geological record are to be expected. In the first place, only a small proportion of the fossil-bearing rocks are actually exposed for our inspection at or near the surface of the earth. By far the greater proportion are hidden below hundreds of thousands of feet of overlying rock. Again, at any particular time, the conditions under which fossilisation can occur, or is likely to occur, will only be found in relatively restricted regions such as marshes, lakes or shallow seas: a great deal of evolution may occur in regions in which no fossils were ever produced or in which, if they were, they have been subsequently destroyed by erosion of the land surface.

It must be remembered also that, although the discontinuities between orders and classes are always striking, they are by no means absolute. In many cases, occasional intermediate types have been found. Thus the first known bird, Archaeopteryx, is, apart from its feathers and wings, more similar to a reptile in its anatomical structure than to a modern bird. Similarly, there are fossils intermediate in many respects between fishes and amphibia, between amphibia and reptiles, and between reptiles and mammals. These always occur approximately (though not always exactly) at the time when the transition from the one class to the other should have taken place. For one reason or another, none of the fossils hitherto discovered, except perhaps Achaeopteryx, can be regarded as on the direct line of descent from one class to another, but they probably lie close to this line. At the least they show that intermediate forms are biologically possible, and they give a general indication of the way in which the transition could have occurred.

Finally, the geological record supports the theory of evolution to the extent that, however inadequate it may be in certain respects, its general features are broadly what would be expected if the theory is true, and are difficult to explain on any other supposition. As we pass from earlier to later rocks, we find among the fossil organisms a continuous tendency towards increasing specialisation on the one hand, and increasing complexity on the other; the latter showing itself most characteristically, among the higher organisms, in an increasing independence of, or mastery of, their environment. Moreover, within any particular class of vertebrates, the earlier representatives of the different orders tend to resemble each other, and their supposed common ancestor, more closely than do the later members; the general pattern of change is that which would be expected if all had diverged from a common origin.

One fact which emerges from the geological record and helps to explain the gaps in it is that macro-evolution has not been a steady process, but tends to proceed in bursts. What happens typically is that at certain critical points a new structural modification is acquired by a particular organism, which enables it to colonise some new, hitherto vacant environment, or to exploit an existing environment in some new way. Once the crucial step has been taken, it is able to spread rapidly with no competition from pre-existing organisms. There are good reasons for supposing that these conditions will encourage an unusually high degree of variability; a greater variety of new forms will be produced which will become adapted to different 'ecological niches'.

Eventually the potentialities of the new environment will have become fairly fully exploited, and then the rate of evolution slows down until some new major advance is achieved. Five critical steps of this sort can be traced in the history of the vertebrates, associated with the first appearance of fishes, amphibians, reptiles, birds and mammals respectively. On a smaller scale, the same sort of sequence of events may be associated with the origin of new orders and families. It is therefore reasonable to suppose that the earlier stages of any big evolutionary advance will be passed through more rapidly than the later ones, and that they will be correspondingly more poorly represented in the geological record. At the present time, the world seems to be in a quiescent period, so much so that some biologists, such as Julian Huxley, believe that macro-evolution is now complete, except that the human race is capable of further major evolution provided that man himself will take a hand in the process. But most biologists would doubt whether there is any good evidence for this view.

The most important evidence for macro-evolution is derived from comparative anatomy and physiology. It is found that all members of any particular phylum are built upon a substantially similar plan, and the similarity becomes progressively more exact among the members of the class, order and family. All vertebrates, for instance, have heart, liver, kidneys, red blood, brain and nervous system conforming to the same fundamental pattern; all have basically similar skeletons in which it can be said, with some qualifications, that each individual bone of any vertebrate animal corresponds to, or is homologous with, some particular bone in every other. In many cases this remains true even when, in some particular species, the bone in question has ceased to fulfil any useful function; it may still occur in a vestigial stage, presumably as an inheritance from some remote ancestor. Thus the rudimentary tail bones in man, and the legs of the python, appear to be genuinely vestigial structures with no value to their possessors. It should be added, however, that there is little evidence of any common structural plan as between the different phyla and no geological evidence of any linkage between them. It would therefore be quite plausible to suppose that some or all of them had evolved independently from distinct prototypes. As a working hypothesis, however, the theory of a single common origin for all phyla seems at present to be more satisfactory.

Evolution and Natural Selection

Before we consider the weight of evidence in favour of the theory of evolution we must draw attention to the distinction between evolution and natural selection. There is no doubt that in Darwin's theory natural selection played a prominent part. In fact the full title of his *Origin of Species* is *The Origin of Species by Means of Natural Selection or the Preservation of Favoured Races in the Struggle for Life.* The idea that favourable variations would tend to be preserved came to him by reading Malthus on Population but contrary to Malthus he applied the idea not only to man but to the whole animal and vegetable kingdoms. His *Origin of Species* could be conceived as a book which establishes and then works out systematically and in great detail the consequences of this principle. He deals with this central idea of his book in the fourth chapter but the previous chapters are already directed to it by way of preparation. As he himself explains in the Introduction of his book:

> ...I shall devote the first chapter of this Abstract to Variation under Domestication. We shall thus see that a large amount of hereditary modification is at least possible; and, what is equally or more important, we shall see how great is the power of man in accumulating by his Selection successive slight variations. I will

then pass on to the variability of species in a state of nature; but I shall, unfortunately, be compelled to treat this subject far too briefly, as it can be treated properly only by giving long catalogues of facts. We shall, however, be enabled to discuss what circumstances are most favourable to variation. In the next chapter the Struggle for Existence amongst all organic beings throughout the world, which inevitably follows from the high geometrical ratio of their increase, will be considered. This is the doctrine of Malthus, applied to the whole animal and vegetable kingdoms. As many more individuals of each species are born than can possibly survive; and as, consequently, there is a frequently recurring struggle for existence, it follows that any being, if it vary however slightly in any manner profitable to itself, under the complex and sometimes varying conditions of life, will have a better chance of surviving, and thus be *naturally selected*. From the strong principle of inheritance, any selected variety will tend to propagate its new and modified form.

Yet Darwin never claimed that evolution can be explained solely by natural selection. He emphasised again and again that in his opinion natural selection was not the exclusive means of modification; it was only one factor, and according to him the most important factor among many, by which we can understand how evolution works.

It is therefore important to keep these two concepts 'Evolution' and 'Natural Selection' distinct, and when we talk about the weight of evidence in favour of evolution, we intend to prescind from the different question whether the principle of natural selection is adequate, and how adequate, for the explanation of evolution.

What should be the judgment of a reasonably detached critic on the theory of evolution? Has it been satisfactorily established or not? Before answering this question we must ask ourselves what sort of evidence we can reasonably require. We cannot hope to have the same sort of certainty of its truth as we can of propositions such as '3 + 4 = 7', or 'Paris is the capital of France'. In everyday life, and also in science, we accept without question innumerable beliefs which, although highly probable, cannot be proved with absolute certainty, and it would be foolish to refuse assent to evolution on the ground that some impossibly high criterion of verification had not yet been achieved. The question is then: what sort of confirmation can be obtained, and what degree of acceptance does this justify? The problem is complicated by the fact that evolution can be judged according to two different criteria: as history or as a scientific theory. The distinction is one of degree rather than of kind, but it is sufficiently important to deserve further consideration. The historian, judging of some past event, will look in the first place for direct evidence that it did or did not happen: archaeological remains, contemporary documents, and so on. The scientist on the other hand, when he propounds a theory, does not generally begin by asking: is this theory true in an absolute sense? What he wants to know is whether it is consistent with the known facts, whether it enables him to integrate and co-ordinate the phenomena into a single, simple, intelligible pattern; whether it suggests fruitful lines for future research or makes predictions which are subsequently verified; whether it is superior in these respects to any alternative theory which might be suggested. In so far as it fulfils these conditions it is a good theory. The distinction in method is by no means absolute. The historian must fall back on theory in order to fill in details, and especially in dealing with obscure or badly documented regions of his subject; the scientist can make many positive assertions of fact and he can also claim that a theory which fits the facts well has a real likelihood of being true in an absolute sense. Nevertheless it does correspond to a real difference of approach.

Now, judged by the standards of the historian, macro-evolution does not show up too well. The direct evidence that it has happened is scanty, and lets us down at a number of critical points. On the other hand, judged as a scientific theory, it comes through with flying colours and is, indeed, indispensable to the biologist. It fulfils all the conditions of a good theory. It enables him to link up a vast range of diverse phenomena in geology, comparative anatomy and physiology, embryology, genetics and natural history. It has made predictions which have subsequently been verified, as for instance that there must be fossil organisms intermediate in structure between man and the apes, and between one class of vertebrates and another. It seems, moreover, in the present state of knowledge, to be the only theory which can serve any useful purpose. The only alternative seems to be Special Creation – the theory that each species or family, or whatever it may be, was specially created by God either out of nothing or, in some unknown but miraculous way, out of pre-existing matter. This is not a scientific theory and is scientifically not useful. Primarily, what the scientist asks of a theory is that it should enable him to understand why things happen in this way rather than that: to select from the infinite number of possible patterns of events just one, or a limited group, to which the actual events conform. Now the difficulty about Special Creation is that it is consistent with almost any conceivable pattern of events. A Special Creationist could argue, for instance, that the first man was created about 4,000 B.C. and that all the apparent relics of earlier men – Stonehenge, the Altamira Cave-paintings, the skeletons of Neanderthal Man etc. – were directly created by God *in situ* without any human agency, for God is free

25

to act as he pleases. But there is a limit to this line of argument. To suppose that each species has been separately created would be to make nonsense of the greater part of modern biology, and would suggest that the world is fundamentally deceptive and unintelligible. Most biologists would be inclined to say that the same applies where macro-evolution is concerned, at least up to and including the common origin of all members of each phylum. And it is, undoubtedly, very difficult to understand why, for instance, God should have created even a few intermediate forms between one class and another at just about the time when the transition, on evolutionary theory, should have occurred or why forms intermediate in bodily structure between man and the apes should have been created shortly before man appeared on the earth.

Whatever may be the position at the present time, it is certain that the great majority of biologists will not be prepared to abandon the scientific search for the explanation of the biological history of the world unless and until it becomes clear that the quest is hopeless, and this is certainly not the case now. So long as the theory of evolution is the only available natural explanation of the biological history of the world, it will continue to be accepted as a matter of course, both by Catholic and non-Catholic biologists.

CHAPTER 2

EVOLUTION AS A THEOLOGICAL PROBLEM

I. A HISTORICAL NOTE

The theory of evolution raised a number of important theological questions. It directly challenged the story of creation in Genesis which seemed to teach that each species had been independently created. More importantly, if indirectly, it gave a weapon to those who thought that a purely naturalistic explanation of man's origin is the correct one. The naturalists used the theory of evolution to 'prove' that man, like any other animal, is the product of natural selection and not a child of God. The origin of his existence is to be sought not in an all-powerful and wise Creator who guides him by his providence but in random variations, mutations and the preservation of favourable modifications. For us this crude mixing of scientific and theological questions about the origin of man may appear to be very naive but a hundred years ago the controversy prompted by Darwin's theory was characterised by this fusion and confusion of scientific and theological questions. Alvar Ellegård in his book *Darwin and the General Reader* (Göteborg University Press, 1958), in which he examines the British periodical literature between 1859 and 1872, clearly shows that the reaction to Darwin was a much more complex affair than has generally been recognised. There were three points at issue: the theory of evolution as such; the theory of natural selection as a sufficient explanation of the process; and the particular question of the origin of man. More or less corresponding to these, there were three main lines of opposition.

The first was based on Scriptural grounds and maintained that evolution of any sort was incompatible with the account of creation given in Genesis which, so it was asserted, requires us to hold that all species of plants and animals were specially created within a period of six days. Leaving out of account, for the moment, the problem of man's origin, this sort of objection was much less widespread than is commonly supposed. It was confined almost entirely to a relatively small group of Evangelical and Nonconformist 'Bible Christians'. The majority of educated people, Catholics included, had abandoned the literal interpretation of the six days earlier in the century, as a result of the great advances which had been made in geological science from about 1800 onwards. There was therefore no great difficulty, from the point of view of Scripture, in abandoning also the doctrine of the special creation of each species, especially as St Augustine had already propounded a quasi-evolutionary theory of creation which was frequently referred to in discussion. Hence the opposition to evolution as such died away relatively quickly, except among a few extremists. Within a few years of the publication of the *Origin of Species* nearly all the organs of public opinion, including most of the religious ones, were prepared to accept it in some form.

Among the Catholic journals the *Dublin Review* gave the *Origin of Species* a favourable review soon after it appeared. The reviewer accepted evolution in principle, although he deplored Darwin's tendency to run too far ahead of his evidence and strongly rejected the suggestion – only vaguely hinted at in the *Origin of Species* – that the theory might explain the origin of man himself. *The Month* did not start publication until 1864, and its first full-length treatment of Darwinism was in 1869, when the famous Catholic biologist Mivart contributed a series of three carefully reasoned articles on the subject. In these again the fact of evolution was fully accepted but it was argued that, in the existing state of scientific knowledge, the theory of Natural Selection could not be regarded as an adequate explanation of the process. *The Rambler* (since defunct) was by far the most hostile of the Catholic reviews and roundly condemned the *Origin of Species,* on its first appearance, as heretical. *The Tablet* hardly noticed Darwin until it came under Dr Vaughan's control in 1868. After this it became generally hostile, while not claiming that there was any clear theological objection to evolution as applied to organisms below the level of man.

Objections on Grounds of Natural Theology

The second main line of opposition arose on grounds of Natural Theology. During the first half of the nineteenth century theologians, especially Protestant ones, had leaned heavily on arguments from design in nature, in order to prove the existence and Providence of God. These arguments generally took the form: science cannot fully explain the evidences of design in the physical world, therefore we must postulate the existence of God in order to supplement the deficiency. Geology, for instance, cannot explain how the earth's crust developed from a formless chaos of rock into its present orderly and habitable condition; hence we conclude that God has intervened miraculously in the past, producing a series of cataclysms which moulded the surface according to his will. Paleontology cannot explain the origin of organic species; hence they must have been miraculously created. Biology cannot explain the wonderful adaptations of things to their environment, the marvels of instinctive behaviour and so on; hence these are a proof of the continuing direct providential interposition of God in the functioning of the world even at the sub-human level. It

29

was not only the professional theologians who used these arguments; they were developed with equal or greater enthusiasm by many of the leading scientists who regarded themselves almost as official interpreters of the ways of God to man in the natural order. So firmly entrenched had this system of apologetics become that when Darwin argued that the origin and adaptation of organisms might be capable of a purely natural explanation, the very foundations of religion seemed to many people to have been undermined. This undoubtedly explains the violence of the immediate reaction against Darwin, the fact that many scientists were initially among his bitterest opponents, and the fact that Catholics and High Anglicans (who relied less exclusively on this type of 'physico-theology') took the situation more calmly than many of their Protestant brethren. The Catholic attitude to evolution seems to have become notably more hostile during the eighteen-nineties than it had been twenty or thirty years earlier. The unfortunate results of this change, which was probably due to the modernist crisis, are apparent in the attitude of too many Catholics towards the natural sciences even today. Though the opposition to evolution as such abated fairly quickly, nevertheless the idea that Natural Selection is a denial of God's Providence dies much harder; many people still find it difficult to accept that God can exercise his Providence through the operations of natural law no less than through modifications or suspensions of these operations.

Objections on Grounds of the Spiritual Nature of Man

The last and most serious objection to Darwin concerned the spiritual nature of man. Darwin argued that not only man's body but also his soul – his intellectual and moral capacities – were evolved naturally from his animal ancestors. Some Catholic writers, such as Mivart and, more doubtfully, Hedley, were prepared to admit the possibility that man's body may have evolved from a sub-human animal, but all agreed that his qualities of intellect and free will are different in kind from the instincts and emotions of the brutes, and cannot have evolved from them naturally, as Darwin maintained that they did. This was by far the most important point at issue between Darwin and his opponents as it still is today, and it was always the one on which Catholic controversialists mainly concentrated.

Differing Notions on the Nature of Scientific Method

A final point which emerges from Ellegård's survey is that, even apart from the question of man, a serious conflict over the principles of Darwinism was inevitable since the two sides held irreconcilably different views as to the nature of scientific method. The traditionalists argued that the accepted physico-theological teaching, with its insistence on miraculous creations, direct interpositions of Providence and so on, was in possession of the field and ought not to be abandoned or disturbed without very cogent evidence. They pointed out that Darwin had not been able to produce any conclusive arguments in favour of his own theories; hence his action in throwing over the established order of things was irresponsible and reprehensible. The Darwinians, on the other hand, took their stand on the principle that explanations in terms of physical law are always to be preferred to those which postulate special divine interventions. Hence natural selection, as the only available theory which conforms to this criterion, is in possession unless it can be proved incorrect. Today it is clear that the Darwinian policy, provided that it accepts certain limitations in the case of man, is the more fruitful. It is healthier not only for science but also for theology. The nineteenth-century apologetics which sought to prove the existence of God from the inability of current science to explain certain phenomena, was essentially unstable. If apologetics is to be based on the fact that there are some things in the physical order which science cannot explain, then every advance by the scientists implies a corresponding retreat by the theologians. As the gaps in our scientific knowledge gradually close, physico-theology becomes involved in a rearguard action, surrendering one position after another until the whole basis of religion appears to be undermined. The process is undignified and it can be a source of grave scandal to those whose faith is weak. It inevitably produces conflicts between science and religion, to the detriment of both. Darwin and many of his followers undoubtedly went too far when they asserted that man's intellectual and voluntary activities are similar in kind to the instinctive and emotional behaviour of the lower animals, and on this point there must always be conflict between theology and a purely materialist science. But within its own sphere science has a right to its autonomy, which should not be surrendered in the supposed interests of apologetics. The recognition of this fact came slowly and with difficulty; it is not yet completely accepted.

II. THE BIBLE

It is not our aim to give here a full account of the biblical notion of creation. For this, any up-to-date book on the subject may be consulted. (See, for example, *The Theology of Creation* by Robert Butterworth S. J. in the present series.) Our purpose is now to sum up two of the major guiding principles by which theologians today deal with the creation-stories in the Bible, and to show that their treatment and conclusions are in no way incompatible with the theory of evolution.

The first, and probably the more important, principle is that the creation stories, as much as the Bible as a whole, intend to convey to us religious truths and not scientific truths. They are a confession of faith in God, the sovereign Lord of all, to whom everything belongs as to its Maker and who upholds everything by his power. Man and his life are under his special care and providence. He sustains him and guides him. Man is wholly dependent on him. The Biblical creation stories proclaim the overall mastery of the God of Israel, who was their Saviour, in the affairs of this world, but do not intend to settle any scientific questions about the origin of the world or man. They do not give us any practical lessons in astronomy, physics, zoology or biology, or in any other branch of positive science. Of course, as has been said before, religious beliefs and truths do not exist in isolation from other beliefs about the world and ourselves; so the creation stories in the Bible express certain views about the world and man. For instance, these stories show the earth as a flat disc above which was the firmament separating the waters below and above it (see Gen 1.7); the sun, the moon and the stars were thought of as lights fixed to the firmament (Gen 1. 14-18). It must be clear to anyone that the views expressed here do not belong to the direct content of revelation. Biblical astronomy but also Biblical zoology and biology have interest for the theologians only in so far as they express the current views on the stars, animals and living organisms at the times when the Biblical stories were composed. Furthermore, it is of some importance to realise that if God wanted to communicate some truths of salvation through men in Sacred Scripture, then these had to be presented in a human fashion, with the basic limitations of human language and in terms of the current views on the world and ourselves; otherwise nobody could have understood the message. It is, therefore, the task of theologians to interpret the Scriptures, and if need be, to separate the content of revelation from the obsolete human views attached to it, and re-present it in terms of present-day views and opinions. The Second Vatican Council in the *Dogmatic Constitution on Divine Revelation* says:

> ...since God speaks in sacred Scripture through man in human fashion, the interpreter of sacred Scripture, in order to see clearly what God wanted to communicate to us, should carefully investigate what meaning the sacred writers really intended, and what God wanted to manifest by means of their words (n. 12).

And a little later:

> In sacred Scripture, therefore, while the truth and holiness of God always remain intact, the marvellous 'condescension' of eternal wisdom is clearly shown, 'that we may learn the gentle kindness of God, which words cannot express, and how far he has gone in adapting his language with thoughtful concern for our weak human nature'. For the words of God, expressed in human language, have been made like human discourse, just as of old the Word of the eternal Father, when he took to himself the weak flesh of humanity, became like other men (n. 13).

The Problem of Literary Forms

But apart from the basic limitations of human language and the inevitable dependence on the contemporary world-picture, there is another limitation that the theologian must keep in mind when dealing with the Bible stories. We refer to the limitation implied in their 'literary forms'. Truths can be expressed in many different ways. For instance, poetry may, and usually does express the truth to be communicated in a different way from that in which a historical textbook does; a novel again differently from a

34

scientific treatise. When we read Gerard Manley Hopkins's poem *The Windhover* in which he represents Christ as a 'dapple-dawn-drawn Falcon', we could not think that he thought Christ to be a bird, nor would we conclude that what he said implied that Christ was not a historical but only a mythological figure. Knowing the literary form (literary genre) of poetry we would understand that the author expressed in a powerful imagery the truth that Christ takes possession of us 'in mastery' and 'brute beauty' just as a falcon hovering in the air suddenly hurls, glides and takes possession of his prey. By this example, of course, we do not intend to insinuate that the Bible stories of creation have the same literary form as Hopkins's poem. We only intended to illustrate that the knowledge of 'literary form' and the interpretation in accordance with it, does not truncate the message to be communicated; on the contrary, it allows a fuller grasp of it. Thus Pope Pius XII in his encyclical *Divino Afflante* (30 September, 1947) says

...frequently the literal sense is not so obvious in the words and writings of ancient oriental authors as it is with the writers of today. For what they intend to signify by their words is determined not only by the laws of grammar or philology, nor merely by the context; it is absolutely necessary for the interpreter to go back in spirit to those remote centuries of the East, and to make proper use of the aids afforded by history, archaeology, ethnology and other sciences, in order to discover what literary forms the writers of that early age intended to use, and did in fact employ. For to express what they had in mind the ancients of the East did not always use the same forms and expressions as we use today; they used those that were current among people of their own time and place; and what these were the exegete cannot determine *a priori*, but only from a careful study of ancient oriental literature. This study has been pursued during the past few decades with greater care and industry than formerly, and has made us better acquainted with the literary forms used in those ancient times, whether in poetical descriptions, or in the formulation of historical facts and events (Dz 3830).

Then a little later Pius XII stresses that a correct understanding of inspiration does not exclude the employment of current literary forms in Sacred Scripture:

...no one who has a just conception of biblical inspiration will be surprised to find that the sacred writers, like the other ancients, employ certain arts of exposition and narrative, certain idioms especially characteristic of the semitic languages (known as 'approximations') and certain hyperbolical and even paradoxical expressions designed for the sake of emphasis. The Sacred Books need not exclude any of the forms of expression that were commonly used in human speech by the ancient people, especially of the East, to convey their meaning, so long as they are in no way incompatible with God's sanctity and truth... In many cases in which the sacred authors are accused of some historical inaccuracy or the inexact recording of some events, it is found to be a question of nothing more than those customary and characteristic forms or styles of narrative which were current in human intercourse among the ancients, and which were in fact quite legitimately and commonly employed. A just impartiality therefore demands that when these are found in the word of God, which is expressed in human language for man's sake, they should be no more stigmatized as error than when similar expressions are employed in daily use. Thus a knowledge and careful appreciation of ancient modes of expression and literary forms and styles will provide a solution to many of the objections made against the truth and historical accuracy of Holy Writ... (Dz 3830).

The same teaching has been repeated by the Second Vatican Council in the *Dogmatic Constitution on Revelation:*

Those who search out the intention of the sacred writers must, among other things, have regard for 'literary forms'. For truth is proposed and expressed in a variety of ways, depending on whether the text is history of one kind or another, or whether its form is that of prophecy, poetry, or some other type of speech. The interpreter must investigate what meaning the sacred writer intended to express and actually expressed in particular circumstances as he used contemporary literary forms in accordance with the situation of his own time and culture. For the correct understanding of what the sacred author wanted to assert, due attention must be paid to the customary and characteristic styles of perceiving, speaking and narrating which prevailed at the time of the sacred writer, and to the customs men normally followed at that period in their everyday dealings with one another (n. 12).

Now, it is well known that the problem of the literary form of the creation-stories is a very difficult one. These stories combine different traditions which are separated by several centuries. The first account of creation (Gen 1.1-2.4a) represents a much later tradition than the second account (Gen 2.4b-25). Both of them, but especially the first one, use elements which can be found in oriental creation-myths. The comparison of the Biblical creation stories with a number of highly mythological accounts of creation not only shows the dependence of the former on the latter, but brings out vital differences between them. The biblical stories, for instance, consistently manifest a faith which is monotheistic, and do not allow any dualistic conception of good and evil in the work of creation. But whatever we may think of the difficult and not wholly solved problem of the literary form of biblical creation stories, it seems to be indisputable that the sacred authors did not intend to give us a simple historical account. Keeping in mind this and our previous remark that the Bible is a book of salvation and not a book of science, we may reasonably say that the theory of evolution at least in principle is not incompatible with the accounts of creation in the Bible.

Two Cautions

Having said this, we immediately would like to add two cautions. First, the separation of the religious questions from the scientific ones in regard to the origin of man can go too far. Some theologians seem to think that since the biblical teaching of creation is not a lesson in cosmogony, scientific questions about the origin of world and man are completely irrelevant to it. This seems to be an extreme position and a mistaken one at that. The fact that several scientific theories of cosmogony and biology are compatible with the biblical notion of creation does not warrant the conclusion that none is incompatible with it. It is quite conceivable that some scientific theories, not in themselves but by implication, are opposed to the position which is expressed in the Bible. If, for instance, a scientific theory allows only a purely materialistic view of man's nature it would by implication be contrary to the teaching of the Bible. Moreover, the total separation of the scientific field from the theological one raises serious questions about the cognitive status of religious beliefs and their relevance in the present world.

Secondly, the fact that the problem of the literary form of the creation stories in the Bible has not yet been solved completely does not mean that we may interpret these creation stories in any arbitrary way. Every interpretation must fit in with the content and other elements of the Scripture as a whole. In addition to this, serious attention should be given to the living tradition of the Church.

...since Holy Scripture must be read and interpreted according to the same Spirit by whom it was written, no less serious attention must be given to the content and unity of the whole of Scripture, if the meaning of the sacred texts is to be correctly brought to light. The living tradition of the whole Church must be taken into account along with the harmony which exists between elements of faith. It is the task of exegetes to work according to these rules toward a better understanding and explanation of the meaning of sacred Scripture, so that through preparatory study the judgment of the Church may mature. For all of what has been said about the way of interpreting Scripture is subject finally to the judgment of the Church, which carries out the divine commission and ministry of guarding and interpreting the word of God (Second Vatican Council on *Divine Revelation*) (12).

This is why now we intend to examine the most important documents of the Church which bear on the theory of evolution.

III. OFFICIAL TEACHING OF THE CHURCH

The Church has no direct dogmatic pronouncement on evolution as a scientific theory; in fact she would be incompetent to issue one. Nevertheless, the Church as the guardian of faith has the competence and duty to defend the doctrine of revelation even if this may involve certain judgments about the conclusions of a scientific theory.

Dogmatic Pronouncements

The fundamental principles governing the relationship between revealed doctrine known by faith and secular knowledge known by reason have been laid down by the First Vatican Council, Third Session (1870) in the *Dogmatic Constitution on the Catholic Faith*. The teaching includes the important statement that there can be no real contradiction between faith and reason.

The Catholic Church with one consent has also ever held and holds that there is a twofold order of knowledge, distinct both in principle and also in object: in principle, because our knowledge in the one is by natural reason, and in the other by divine faith; in object, because, besides those things which natural reason can attain, there are proposed to our belief mysteries hidden in God, which, unless divinely revealed, cannot be known... (Dz 3015).

...although faith is above reason, there can never be any real discrepancy between faith and reason, since the same God who reveals mysteries and infuses faith has bestowed the light of reason on the human mind, and God cannot deny himself, nor can truth ever contradict truth. The false appearance of such a contradiction is mainly due, either to the dogma of faith not having been understood and expounded according to the mind of the Church, or to the inventions of opinion having been taken for the verdicts of reason. 'We define, therefore, that every assertion contrary to a truth of enlightened faith is utterly false' [Lateran V].

Further, the Church, which together with the apostolic office of teaching has received a charge to guard the deposit of faith, derives from God the right and duty of proscribing false science (1 Tim 6.20), lest any should be deceived by philosophy and vain fallacy (Col 2.8). Therefore, all faithful Christians are not only forbidden to defend, as legitimate conclusions of science, such opinions as are known to be contrary to the doctrines of faith, especially if they have been condemned by the Church, but are altogether bound to account them as errors which put on the fallacious appearance of truth.

And not only can faith and reason never be opposed to one another, but they are of mutual aid one to the other; for right reason demonstrates the foundation of faith and, enlightened by its light, cultivates the science of things divine; while faith frees and guards reason from errors, and furnishes it with manifold knowledge. So far, therefore, is the Church from opposing the cultivation of human arts and sciences, that in many ways it helps and promotes it. For the Church neither ignores nor despises the benefits to human life which result from the arts and sciences, but confesses that as they come from God, the Lord of all science, rightly used they lead to God by the help of his grace. Nor does the Church forbid that each of these sciences in its sphere should make use of its own principles and its own method; but, while recognizing this just liberty, it stands watchfully on guard, lest sciences, setting themselves against the divine teaching, or transgressing their own limits, should invade and disturb the domain of faith (Dz 3017-19).

When we try to understand the exact meaning of these passages we have to keep in mind the errors they sought to refute. These were rationalism and materialism on the one hand, traditionalism and fideism on the other. The Council Fathers have taken a steady middle course between these two heretical positions. They allowed different approaches to truth, one by reason, one by faith, yet they affirmed the final unity of truth. The ultimate reason why there cannot be any real contradiction between faith and reason is that truth can never contradict truth: God is the source of both faith and reason.

We would like to draw attention again to the teaching of

the final unity of truth because there is a tendency in the present time to isolate the realm of faith too radically from the realm of reason. It is not infrequently said that there is no point of contact between scientific and theological discourses; each has its own 'language-game' with special grammar and syntax; hence it is futile to attempt the construction of any general framework of truths, which would accommodate both. The teaching of the First Vatican Council seems to exclude such an extreme position.

It is of some importance that according to the Council document the 'false appearance' of contradiction between faith and reason may be due not only to 'false science' or 'inventions of opinions having been taken for the verdicts of reason' but also to 'dogmas of faith not having been understood' properly (see Dz 3017). Thus the apparent conflict between faith and reason may provide an opportunity for a better understanding of our faith.

Official but Non-Dogmatic Documents

Apart from the dogmatic teaching of Vatican I, the Provincial Council of Cologne (1860), the encyclical *Providentissimus Deus* (1893) by Leo XIII, the *Decree of the Biblical Commission* in 1909, the encyclicals *Divino Afflante Spiritu* (1943) and *Humani Generis* (1950) by Pius XII, bear on the theory of evolution. None of these documents has the guarantee of infallibility, yet they contain the teaching of the official ecclesiastical authority, demanding respect and consideration.

The Provincial Council of Cologne (1860) was convoked to counter the heretical views of Hermes and Günther. It issued a decree on the origins of the human race and human nature which includes the following statement:

Our first parents were immediately made by God.

Thus we declare plainly opposed to the Holy Scripture and to faith the opinion of those who go so far as to say that man, even as far as his body is concerned, was produced by the spontaneous transformation of the less perfect into the more perfect, successively, ultimately ending in the human. (Titulus IV, cap. 14)

And a little later we find in the same chapter:

Those... who say that we do not know the origin of the human race or those who deny that the whole human race has been propagated from Adam, are plainly and openly opposed to the Holy Scripture.

A number of theologians think that here is an obvious condemnation of 'spontaneous transformation' and hence evolution. Others (see e.g. C. Messenger, *Evolution and Theology* p. 226) point out that, since such decrees should always be interpreted strictly, the document does not condemn evolution as such but 'spontaneous transformation' that would explain the origin of man without a recourse to an intelligent Creator. These theologians also add that the pronouncement of the Council of Cologne remained an isolated instance and later the Biblical Commission adopted a more moderate formula.

The encyclical *Providentissimus Deus* (1893) by Pope Leo XIII reiterates the teaching of Vatican I that there can be no real contradiction between Scripture and the findings of science, and gives some guidance as to what to do if still there is disagreement:

No real disaccord can exist between the theologian and the scientist provided each keeps within his own limits and follows the warning of St Augustine to beware of 'affirming anything rashly, and the unknown as known'. If nevertheless there is disagreement, the same Doctor proposes a summary rule for the theologian: 'Whatever they are able to demonstrate about nature by true proofs, let us show that it is not contrary to our Scriptures. But whatever they propose in any books of theirs which is contrary to our Scriptures – that is to say, to the Catholic faith – let us also show, if we are at all able, or at all events let us believe without any doubt that it is most false.' In order to understand the justness of this rule it should be remembered, in the first place, that the sacred writers, or more truly 'the Spirit of God who spoke through them', did not wish to teach men these truths (that is to say, the inward constitution of visible objects) which would not help any to salvation; and that for this reason, rather than apply themselves directly to the investigation of nature, they sometimes describe and treat the objects themselves either in language to some extent figurative, or as the common manner of speech of the period required, and indeed still requires nowadays in everyday life in regard to many things, even among the most learned men. And since in popular speech those things are first and chiefly mentioned which fall under the senses, in like manner the sacred writer, as the Angelic Doctor [St Thomas Aquinas speaking of Moses] warns us, 'described those things which appeared to outward sense; that is, those things which God himself, in addressing men, signified after the human fashion so as to be understood by them'... (Dz 3287-88).

There is little need to add any comment here. *Providentissimus Deus* represents the first serious treatment, in an official document, of the problems raised by biblical criticism. Many of the ideas and themes of the encyclical were developed fifty years later by Pope Pius XII in his encyclical *Divino Afflante Spiritu* (1943).

At the beginning of this century, on 30 October, 1902, Pope Leo XIII founded the *Biblical Commission* to advance biblical studies and to decide on unsettled questions. On 18 November, 1907 Pope Pius X granted the same authority to the decisions of the Biblical Commission as those of Roman Congregations. In an answer concerning the historical character of the first chapters of Genesis, the Biblical Commission passed the following decree: (30 June, 1909).

Question 3. Whether in particular the historical meaning of words may be called in doubt when it is a question of the facts narrated in these chapters which touch upon the foundations of the Christian religion, such as, for example, the creation of all things by God at the beginning of time, the particular creation of man, the formation of the first woman from the first man, the unity of the human race, the original happiness of the first parents in a state of justice, integrity and immortality, the commandment given by God to man to test his obedience, the transgression of the divine commandments at the instigation of the devil in the form of a serpent, the ejection of our first parents from their primal state of innocence, and finally the promise of the Redeemer to come. Answer: No (Dz 3514).

This decree was directed against certain exegetes who interpreted the first chapters of Genesis purely allegorically denying *any* historical sense to them. The decision does not assert that the chapters of Genesis contain history in the modern sense, nor does it say that the problem of their literary form has been solved. In it there is nothing against the general doctrine of evolution. In fact the careful wording of the decree suggests that the intention of the Commission was to leave the question of evolution open.

In regard to the intention of the Commission some light is thrown by the Secretary of the Commission in a letter addressed to Cardinal Suhard, Archbishop of Paris on the 16th of January, 1948. Apparently, Cardinal Suhard asked the Commission whether the time had not come to make a new decree on the 'literary form' of the first chapters of Genesis. In a reply the Secretary of the Commission quoted *Divino Afflante Spiritu* on the liberty of the Catholic exegetes, and called attention to the need for restraint on the part of those who regarded everything new with suspicion. Then, in the following passage, he invites a broad interpretation of the historicity of the events related in the first chapters of Genesis:

The question of the literary forms in the first eleven chapters of Genesis is very complicated and obscure. These literary forms do not correspond to any of our classic categories and cannot be judged in the light of Graecô-Latin or modern literary forms. Their historicity can be neither affirmed nor denied *en bloc* without unjustifiably applying to them the rules of a literary *genre* in which they cannot be classified... To declare *a priori* that the accounts in them do not contain history in the modern sense of the word would easily lead to the misunderstanding that they contain no history in any sense of the word, whereas they relate in a simple and colourful language suitable to the mentality of a not very developed mankind the basic truths underlying the economy of salvation, and at the same time the popular description of the origins of the human race and the chosen people (Dz 3864).

Pius XII in his encyclical *Humani Generis* (1950) referred to this letter of the Secretary of the Biblical Commission and repeated its teaching:

It was clearly laid down in that letter that the first eleven chapters of Genesis, although it is not right to judge them by modern standards of historical composition, such as would be applied to the great classical authors, or to the learned of our day, do nevertheless come under the heading of history; in what exact sense, it is for the further labours of the exegete to determine. These chapters have a naive, symbolical way of talking, well suited to the understanding of a primitive people. But they do disclose to us certain important truths, upon which the attainment of our eternal salvation depends, and they do also give a popularly-written description of how the human race, and the chosen people in particular, came to be. It may be true that these old writers of sacred history drew some of their material from the stories current among the people of their day. So much may be granted; but it must be remembered on the other side that they did so under the impulse of divine inspiration, which preserved them from all error in selecting and assessing the material they used (Dz 3898).

The same encyclical *Humani Generis* (1950) is the only official document in which the phrase 'doctrine of evolution' occurs:

Thus the teaching of the Church leaves the doctrine of evolution an open question, as long as it confines its speculations to the development of the human body from other living matter already in existence. (That souls are immediately created by God is a view which the Catholic faith imposes on us.) In the present state of scientific and theological opinion, this question may be legitimately canvassed by research, and by discussion between those who are expert in both subjects. At the same time, the reasons for and against either view must be weighed and judged with all seriousness, fairness and restraint; and there must be a readiness on all sides to accept the decision of the Church, as being entrusted by Christ with the task of interpreting the Scriptures aright, and the duty of safeguarding the doctrines of the faith. There are some who take rash advantage of this liberty of debate, by treating the subject as if the whole matter were closed – as if the discoveries hitherto made, and the arguments based on them, were sufficiently certain to prove, beyond doubt, the development of the human body from other living matter already in existence. They forget, too, that there are certain references to the subject in the sources of divine revelation, which call for the greatest caution and prudence in discussing it (Dz 3896).

Perhaps the most significant statement of *Humani Generis* is that it declares the doctrine of evolution an open question with certain qualifications. These qualifications intend to safeguard two major dogmas of our faith, the spiritual nature of man and original sin. The theory of evolution raises some problems, by implication, in regard to the understanding of these two dogmas of our faith, to which we turn our attention in the next chapter.

Conclusion

We may conclude this section by saying that the Church, in her official teaching, has never condemned the theory of evolution as such. Yet, it would be futile to deny that her officials for a long period had a hostile attitude to the theory. The limitations imposed on the publication of the writings of certain theologians such as Teilhard de Chardin testify to this hostile official attitude which, no doubt, was aggravated by the modernist crisis and its after-effects. However, since about 1950 there has been a marked change of atmosphere. Catholic authors put forward ideas accepting man's evolutionary origins without any interference on the part of ecclesiastical authority. Indeed, some of them may have influenced the text of the *Pastoral Constitution on the Church in the Modern World* issued by the Second Vatican Council (4 December 1963). In article 5 the following sentence occurs: 'Thus the human race has passed from a rather static concept of reality to a more dynamic, evolutionary one', and later in article 74 we find the expression 'dynamically conceived common good'. The editor of *The Documents of Vatican II* observes in a footnote: 'The reference to dynamic evolutionary forces here is perhaps one reason why some critics early objected to the influence of the thought of Pierre

Teilhard de Chardin on the document' (p. 204).

Undoubtedly the Magisterium takes now a much more open and less cautious position in regard to the theory of evolution. Through the deeper understanding of the Bible narratives and of the nature of religious truth, man's evolutionary origin no longer seems to threaten the basic dogmas of our faith. There are, however, two outstanding problems which must be discussed in the light of evolution: original sin and the special creation of the soul.

CHAPTER 3

THEOLOGICAL IMPLICATIONS OF EVOLUTION

The Incompatibility of Scientific and Older Theological Accounts of Human Origins

It must be realized quite clearly that the acceptance of evolution implies a considerable change in the theological understanding of the origin of man which we have inherited from the Middle Ages. According to this, the world was created a few thousand years ago, in six days, each living species being separately created. The first man, Adam, was formed from clay, miraculously transformed, and put into a planted garden of Eden. Eve was made from one of Adam's ribs and given to him as a helper and wife. Adam was the ideal prototype of humanity, with perfect beauty, health, psychophysical integrity and intelligence. God revealed to him all the truths of theology, philosophy and natural science which could be helpful to him in this life on earth; according to St Thomas he had all the knowledge which man is naturally capable of attaining, apart from such irrelevant details as the number of pebbles on the bed of a river. He was equipped with a fully developed language to express his knowledge.

So long as he was faithful to God's commands he would be preserved by a special Providence from all disease, accident, natural disaster, suffering and death. Similarly, if Adam had been faithful, all his descendants would have been born into this world with the same privileges. All this was, of course, in addition to, and in view of, the primary and essential gift that he, and all his descendants, would have been constituted from the beginning in a state of grace, in friendship with God, and with an orientation towards the Beatific Vision.

Adam's transgression brought this Paradisal state of affairs to an end. Man became at enmity with God and a slave to the devil. He lost his integrity; he became subject to suffering and death. The harmony of his nature was destroyed. Henceforth all men are born with a nature intrinsically disordered from the moment of conception and with a stain of guilt passed on to them from Adam, through their parents, by the process of physical generation. They can do nothing of their own power to restore themselves to a state of grace and friendship with God. This can only be effected through the redeeming power of Christ.

According to the modern scientific view of human origins, the earth came into existence several thousands of millions of years ago. By a slow process of evolution the various species of plants and animals gradually came into being. One particular group of animals – the primates – developed a particularly complex brain and nervous system, and eventually one branch of this group evolved into man. The earliest men were very primitive, with smaller brain-capacity and a more ape-like appearance than modern man. Their culture and technological achievements were rudimentary, and it is to be presumed that their knowledge of natural science, philosophy and theology were equally so.

Polygenism versus monogenism

Science gives no direct knowledge of the actual transition from the non-human to the human level, but the general principles of genetics and comparative anatomy would lead one to suppose that man's origin was polygenetic and not monogenetic, i.e. the transition from sub-human to human would have occured repeatedly in several individuals, and so the race was not generated from a single human pair.

The reasons why science assumes a polygenetic origin of mankind can be reduced to two:

a) One human pair would be too narrow a base genetically for mankind and would imply a genetic weakness of an inbreeding type. (For further reading see, for instance, *Human Origin and Genetics,* by A. Alexander in *Clergy Review,* vol. 49 (1964) pp. 344-356).

b) The emergence of any new species normally takes place in numerous individuals about the same time and, scientifically, there is nothing which would make us believe that in the case of *Homo sapiens* there was an exception from this general rule. Indeed, comparative anatomy strongly suggests that *Homo sapiens* appeared essentially the same way as any other species.

On the other hand, most scientists consider that the human species did evolve within a single group at a certain limited time and place. This theory is called monophyletism and is opposed to polyphyletism, the theory that mankind emerged through several transitions from sub-human to human populations in different parts of the earth at different times. Polyphyletism is accepted by few scientists today; there is no evidence for it and it is difficult to reconcile with the normal biological processes of biological speciation.

As the weight of scientific opinion in favour of polygenism became stronger, the theologians began to see that there is a genuine difficulty in accepting Adam as the sole progenitor of the human race. To meet this difficulty new theological interpretations of 'Adam' were put forward, picturing Adam as a group, leader of a group, or a 'corporate' representative of an original human population (See, for instance, *Il peccato originale in prospectiva evolutionistica* by Z. Alszeghi and M. Flick in *Gregorianum* (1966) pp. 201-225, or a shorter account by the same authors, *Original Sin and Evolution* in *The Tablet,* 17 September 1966, pp. 1039-41). These 'compromise' theories could hardly avoid a certain artificiality, and, in some sense, were similar to those juridical representation theories – well known in scholastic manuals since the sixteenth century – according to which Adam, a single individual, was given a mandate 'by divine decree' to act on behalf of the whole mankind. (See e.g. J. F. Sagüés: *De Deo creante et elevante, Sac. Theol. Summa,* BAC 2.2)

Of the relationship of the first man to God science can tell us nothing. It cannot confirm or deny that the first man or men were constituted in a state of sanctifying grace or that this was lost by some primeval transgression. It can, however, assert that the traditional picture of Eden would have involved so radical an interference with the ordinary laws of nature as to have rendered the world quite unintelligible. Thus there can be no doubt that the scientific and the older theological accounts of human origin are incompatible with each other.

I. ORIGINAL SIN

We have argued in the previous chapter that the Church in her official teaching never condemned the theory of evolution as such and the cautious, and at times perhaps hostile attitude on the part of the Church towards evolution could be explained by her earnestness to safeguard two major dogmas of our faith: the spiritual nature of man, and original sin. Hence if evolution is accepted then a new theological understanding of these two basic dogmas is called for. The work has been started, and those who want to be sufficiently informed should read the publications of Rahner, Schoonenberg, Hulsbosch and others (See Bibliography). Here, we must be content with a bare outline of the general direction of the different attempts towards a solution. First we discuss original sin and then the creation of the soul.

Every human being is born into this world with a nature
that is imperfectly integrated and inadequately oriented towards its final end. 'Before' the grace of Christ, man's state
is a state of separation from God, a state of darkness, futili-
ty and disorder. This, however, was not God's original plan.
He, from the beginning, called man to integrity and fulfilment. The disorder came through the sinful act of Adam.
He is not an individual who lived on earth at a remote period of history but the concrete, individual representation of
every man. He is, therefore, not a historical figure in the
sense in which, for example, Napoleon is; nor is he a figure of
pure imagination for *what he represents is realized histori-
cally in every human being.* Similarly, Adam's sin is the
concrete, symbolic representation of *every human sin.* It
can be viewed under two aspects: in its origin and in its
consequences. In its origin, it is a sinful personal act carry-
ing with it personal guilt and remorse; in its consequences it
brings about a *sinful situation,* a state of separation from
God, and leads man to sin personally, and so to make
Adam's sin his own. Once it is fully appreciated that the
doctrine of Original Sin speaks primarily of the *present* situation of man, it will become of secondary importance how
this sin is 'inherited' or 'transmitted'. But it seems certain
that the traditional concept of 'biological transmission',
which, incidentally, creates just as many problems as it tries
to solve, is inadequate. It seems more helpful to ground the
'inheritance' of original sin in the social character of man's
life and that of his sins. The individual man in his whole
biological and psychological make-up is to a great extent
produced by the human society in which he lives. He is
born into a situation where sin and evil are a sad reality,
and prior to his own free choice. He 'inherits' a sinful situation simply by being a member of the human family. Pre-

cisely, by being a member of the human family, he shares in the sins, guilt and shame of his fellow-men. He is utterly powerless in face of the mass of mankind's sins and cannot remain unaffected. Thus, God's grace in Christ for him is not only a special free gift, a privilege, but a saving power, a redemption.

The Paradisal state of Adam, including the immunity from concupiscence, suffering and death is not a state that man no longer possesses but one that does not yet exist. It is a state that has been revealed as God's original plan and will for the final state, as a promised and hoped fulfilment of this world, *made operative from the start* in the unfolding, creative activity of God. As Hulsbosch has rightly pointed out, we must not evaluate the act of creation in an evolutionary image with reference to the beginning but with reference to the end:

> The real difference between an idea of creation which functions within a static image of the world, and the idea of creation within an evolutionary image, is this, that within the static image God created *in the beginning,* and with the virtual inclusion of everything which would develop through time out of the cosmic actuality. In the dynamic image attention is directed *to the end.* God creates the world and humanity in Christ. For us who live in time this work of creation is being consummated. The intention of God's creation is consummated in the course of cosmic evolution. This point of departure governs everything in a theology of evolution (*God's Creation* by A. Hulsbosch, p. 30).

To the obvious objection that man cannot fall off from a Paradisal state which he does not yet possess, we may say that by refusing God's will, man frustrates his own completion. Through sin his lack of integrity becomes a sinful absence.

Is this interpretation of original sin contrary to the Bible?

Recent exegetical work has shown that the biblical meanings of the words 'Adam', 'ancestor of', 'descendant of', 'son
of' are far more complex than had been thought. The Hebrew word for man *adam* has both individual and collective
aspects. Accordingly, *adam* can be translated as 'man', 'some
men', 'all men', 'any man whatever', 'human race', 'mankind' or simply 'the man' (Man) the type of all men. The
usage of the word in the collective sense is far more frequent. (Out of the 510 cases in the Old Testament only a
few times is the reference to an individual.) In the Genesis
story of the fall of man (Gen 2.4b-3.24) the word *adam* is
always written with the definite article *ha-adam*, 'the man',
hence it is inaccurately translated by a proper name. In Hebrew to designate clearly an individual man, the expression
ben adam (son of man, member of the human race) must be
used.

In the New Testament 'Adam' occurs only twice when in-
disputably referring to an individual (Lk 3.27; Jude 1.14).
In the famous passage of the letter of Paul to the Romans
(5.12-21) while the author may have thought Adam to be an
individual, the primary meaning of Adam is clearly representative. He typifies the 'old man' representing mankind
unredeemed, and is contrasted to Christ who saves mankind. Adam is therefore the anti-type of Christ. As we have
all sinned 'in Adam', we have all been saved 'in Christ'.

Exegetical work has also shown that the biblical meanings of the expressions 'descendant of', 'son of' should not
be limited to a biological descent. Biblical texts refer to pa-
gans who became Jews as the 'sons of Abraham', to sin-
ners as the 'sons of the devil', to the disciple of a master
as his son. In the third chapter of John's gospel we find a
typical example of 'spiritual generation' and 'birth' (3.6)
where generation in a biological sense cannot arise. Taking
this more general meaning of 'descendant of', there is no

difficulty in itself in interpreting the descent of original sin from Adam independently of a strictly biological descent. In this case the 'son of Adam' or 'descendant of Adam' would mean simply a member of the human race, and the question whether all men originated biologically from one couple (monogenism) or from several (polygenism) becomes irrelevant.

It seems to be true to say that in the light of the results of modern exegesis, the biblical texts do not create any insurmountable difficulties for the new interpretation of original sin. But what about the teaching of the Church?

Magisterium on Original Sin

The first official teaching of the Church on original sin was set out in 418 against Pelagius at the Provincial Council of Carthage, and later confirmed by Pope Zosimus. The Synod, where more than 200 bishops were present, condemned the teaching of Pelagius on grace, which implied an erroneous view on original sin. Pelagius taught that Adam's sin harmed Adam alone, that he was created mortal and would have died whether he had sinned or not, and that children at birth are in the same state as Adam before the Fall. All these teachings are condemned as heretical.

The Second Council of Orange (529), again a Provincial Council, approved later by Pope Boniface II in 531, repeated the teaching of the Synod of Carthage and issued the following decree:

> If anyone maintain that the fall was harmful to Adam alone and not to his descendants, or that only bodily death, which is a punishment of sin, but not sin itself, which is the death of the soul, has passed to the whole of the human race by one man, he ascribes an injustice to God, contradicting the Apostle who says: 'Wherefore as by one man sin entered into this

world, and by sin death; so also death passed upon all men in whom all have sinned' (Rom 5.12) (Dz 372).

One might think that this text clearly includes the assertion that Adam was one individual man and cannot be taken as any man whatever. But the whole context suggests that here the issue was not what 'Adam' referred to, the issue was whether original sin has or has not passed to the whole of the human race. Admittedly, the Council Fathers almost certainly *presupposed* that Adam was one individual man, but since their concern was different, this presupposition is not a part of the dogmatic definition.

The Council of Trent

About a thousand years after the Council of Orange, the *General Council of Trent* dealt with original sin (5th Session, 1546). The occasion was the condemnation of Luther's conception of original sin. The Council Fathers, however, were not content with the rejection of Luther's doctrine. They also reiterated the rejection of the Pelagian heresy. Among these decrees two passages occur, which may seem contrary to the new interpretation of original sin which we have outlined. We give these two passages in full:

If anyone does not confess that Adam, the first man, by his transgression of God's commandment in Paradise immediately lost the sanctity and justice in which he had been constituted, and by the offence of this sin drew upon himself the wrath and indignation of God and the death with which God had threatened him, and with death captivity in the power of him who had the empire of death, that is to say the devil (Heb 2.14), and that the whole Adam by the offence of this sin was changed in body and soul for worse, *anathema sit* (Dz 1511).

This text obviously presupposes in Adam a concrete indi-

58

vidual who lived in Paradise. But here again what we said a few moments ago applies, namely that a presupposition does not necessarily imply an affirmation, and since the Council texts should always be interpreted strictly, the new interpretation which understands in Adam the type of man (everyman) is not incompatible with this text. The Council Fathers were after all the children of their own age: they could not use the results of Biblical exegesis which became available in the twentieth century. Like the sacred authors of the Bible, in expressing religious truths, they used concepts and images that were available in their own time.

The second passage is often quoted as one that implies monogenism, the biological descent of every man from one couple (Adam and Eve):

> If anyone assert that this sin of Adam's, which was one in origin and is passed on by propagation not by imitation, and is in each and proper to each, can be taken away by the powers of human nature or by any remedy other than by the merits of the *one mediator* our Lord Jesus Christ who reconciled us to God by his blood, 'made unto us... justice and sanctification and redemption' (1 Cor 1.30); or deny that this merit of Christ Jesus is applied to adults and to children in the sacrament of baptism duly administered in the Church's form, *anathema sit* (Dz 1513).

At first sight, the expression 'the sin of Adam's, which was one in origin and is passed on by propagation not by imitation' appears, indeed, to imply biological descent from Adam. But if we look at the whole decree we see that the main issue was not the question of biological descent. 'Propagation' is contrasted with 'imitation' which recalls the false conception of Pelagius on original sin, according to which Adam's sin did not really harm every man, and implied a restriction on the universality of Adam's sin. The Council rejected this teaching because it entailed a belittlement of Christ's redemptive work in general, and the uniqueness of his mediatorship in particular. This was the main issue and not the biological descent from Adam, and thus monogenism h.s not been defined by Trent. However, if it could be proved that the Council's teaching on original sin cannot be held without the presupposition of monogenism, then monogenism, though not defined, would be a teaching implicit in the doctrine of original sin and its acceptance binding for all Catholics. In other words, if one could demonstrate that the presupposition of monogenism by the Council Fathers was not merely a historical fact at the time, but was an absolutely (logically) necessary presupposition for the understanding of original sin, then the new interpretation outlined above must be rejected. But at present we have no such proof and it is very unlikely that such a proof would ever be forthcoming. For the theological objections against polygenism have been abundantly developed, and in spite of this, in recent years an increasing weight of theological opinion has been gathering in support of the idea that monogenism is not required in order to explain original sin. It is notable that a leading Roman Catholic theologian, Karl Rahner changed his opinion in the matter. He wrote in 1966: 'Cautious theological reflection enables us to show today that Trent's dogma of original sin does not exclude polygenism. The two can coexist. On this point I have reappraised my own earlier view' (Introduction to *Teilhard and the Creation of the Soul*, by R. North, p. xii).

Apart from the dogmatic teaching of the Church on original sin, two documents have to be considered, which, *prima facie*, seem to exclude polygenism: the *Replies of the Biblical Commission in 1909*, and the encyclical *Humani Generis* (1950).

The Biblical Commission in 1909 enumerated nine facts from the first three chapters of Genesis as pertaining 'among others' to the foundation of Christianity. These were the creation of all things by God at the beginning of time; the peculiar creation of man; the formation of the first woman from the first man; the unity of the human race; the original happiness of our first parents in a state of justice, integrity and immortality; the command given by God to test their obedience; the transgression of this command by the persuasion of the devil in the guise of a serpent; the casting out of our first parents from this state of innocence; the promise of a future redeemer. There can be no doubt that speaking of the 'unity of human race', the Commission meant a strictly monogenistic unity.

Humani Generis and Polygenism

Some forty years later, Pius XII, in his encyclical *Humani Generis,* was much more cautious in his enumeration of historical facts about man's origin. The creation of Eve was not mentioned, nor the serpent. The evolution of the body of the first man was thrown open to discussion, but monogenism was still asserted on the grounds that, without it, there seemed to be no possibility of explaining original sin:

...the teaching of the Church leaves the doctrine of evolution an open question, as long as it confines its speculations to the development, from other living matter already in existence, of the human body...

...There are other conjectures, about polygenism (as it is called), which leave the faithful no such freedom of debate. Christians cannot lend their support to a theory which involved the existence, after Adam's time, of some earthly race of men, truly so called, who were not descended ultimately from him, or else supposes that Adam was the name given to some group of our primordial ancestors. It does not appear how such views can be reconciled with the doctrine of original sin, as this is guaranteed to us by the Church. Original sin is the result of a sin committed, in actual historical fact, by an individual man named

Adam, and it is a quality native to all of us, only because it has been handed down by descent from him (Dz 3987).

Before commenting on these non-infallible documents of the Magisterium, a few words must be said on their theological value. As it has been defined by Vatican I, only dogmatic decrees which are guaranteed by a General Council or by the Pope speaking *ex cathedra* are infallible. However, if a non-infallible document (an encyclical, for instance) repeats an infallible teaching of the Church then this obviously does not cease to be infallible because it has been incorporated into the document. Now, the question of monogenism is a relatively new problem, and it is easy to show that the Church has never intended to make, and thus never made, an infallible decision in the matter. Plainly speaking, this means that Pius XII in *Humani Generis* could have made a mistake. The theological value of such documents refers not so much to the 'true' but to the 'safe' character of its teaching. It decides not whether a teaching is true or false, once and for all, but whether it is safe from the pastoral point of view at a certain point of history. It judges whether a teaching can be affirmed within a determined cultural context without exposing some truth of faith to danger (See Z. Alszeghi, 'Development in the Doctrinal Formulations of the Church concerning the Theory of Evolution' in *Concilium,* Vol. 6, Number 3, June 1967, p. 15).

The cautious wordings of both the Commission ('unity of the human race') and of *Humani Generis* ('*It does not appear* how such views can be reconciled with the doctrine of original sin, as this is guaranteed to us by the Church') may also be relevant here. One may recall that at a certain period of the Middle Ages, the common theological opinion, including that of St Thomas, was against the Immaculate Conception, on the ground that it could not be seen how the universal need for redemption can be reconciled with the teaching that our Lady from the first moment of her existence was immune from original sin. Later, however, when theologians worked out a theology of redemption which could have had its effect before the time of Christ, the difficulties were resolved, and the Immaculate Conception became generally accepted.

For all these reasons, the censures of *Humani Generis* on polygenism should be taken in a limited sense, as indicating guidance from a pastoral point of view at a certain point of history. And because considerable progress has been made since 1950 in the development of the theological understanding of original sin, we think that the question of polygenism, with all due respect to *Humani Generis,* may be treated as an open one.

Clearly, much hard thinking and work will have to be done before a new interpretation of original sin could be generally acceptable, but it does seem to be true to say that the Church is slowly moving at present towards a new interpretation.

II. SPECIAL CREATION OF THE SOUL?

Apart from a new interpretation of original sin, the theory of evolution calls for a new interpretation of the creation of the soul. As we have remarked before, the great controversy on the theory of evolution centred about the spiritual nature of man. The conviction that man has a spiritual nature found expression in the statement: 'Man is different in kind from the brutes because he has a spiritual soul'. The theory of evolution, however, seemed to blur the distinction between men and brutes: the human species became a part of the Animal Kingdom. It seemed that both brutes and men were governed by the same laws not only in their basic biological structures and functions, but also in their developments. Those Christian writers who were, to some extent, sympathetic to the theory admitted that man's body may have been evolved naturally from his animal ancestors, yet they were adamant in asserting that man's intellectual and moral capacities may not be conceived as having developed in and through the evolutionary process. They firmly stated that the *human soul* must have been immediately created by God. This teaching was reaffirmed in *Humani Generis:*

...Thus, the teaching of the Church leaves the doctrine of evolution an open question, as long as it confines its speculations to the development, from other living matter already in existence, of the human body.

(That souls are immediately created by God is a view which the Catholic faith imposes on us.)

It should be noted, incidentally, that *Humani Generis* makes no distinction between the creation of the first human soul and that of every other. Hence the origin of the first human being could be just as 'natural' as the production of any other.

The traditional account of the creation of the soul easily saves the 'essential difference' between man and brutes, and makes the philosophical proofs for the immortality of the soul plausible; nevertheless it poses great difficulties.

The Weakness of the Traditional Account

First, it insinuates a Platonic conception of the soul-body relationship, as if the human body could somehow exist without the human soul. This is contrary to a very ancient theological teaching that soul and body constitute one substantial unity. There is no human body without a human soul, and thus the acceptance of evolution in regard to man's body seems to require a corresponding statement in regard to his soul. And vice versa, the teaching of an immediate creation of the soul seems to require a corresponding statement in regard to his body. As Karl Rahner has rightly pointed out in his book *Hominisation,*

...in actual fact an immediate creation of the soul, if given its full meaning, necessarily implies a statement about man's corporal nature and its coming to be, and a statement about the body as such cannot be anything but a fragment of the real 'pre-history' of the soul. Otherwise man would be divided in the Platonic fashion into soul and body (p. 63).

Secondly, and perhaps more importantly, the traditional account of the special creation of the soul seems to imply a special intervention of God in the chain of finite causes when a human soul is created. This either degrades God to the level of a secondary cause, or makes the creation of a human soul a miracle. Neither of these is acceptable even from the traditional point of view.

In view of these difficulties Karl Rahner has suggested a new theory of 'becoming', in order to explain the creation of the soul. We shall now give a brief summary of his view.

Rahner's Theory

Evolution implies a real 'becoming', a 'self-transcendence': an agent is moving beyond and above its own limits, and produces something that is genuinely greater than itself. Hence evolution appears as a movement from a 'lower' form to a 'higher' one, from a 'less' to a 'more'. But without God a finite being can never give to itself a true increase of being. God however does not destroy the real self-transcendence of a finite being. He should never be conceived as a 'part-cause'. He is the ground of the very possibility of every becoming. Any true development, any new being, is produced not partly by finite causes and partly by God but wholly by the finite causes in virtue of the evolutionary dynamism God endows them with. For this reason God's creative activity is not an item in our experience; it is always mediated to us through finite things. Yet, every fi-

65

nite being, in its existence and development, depends utterly and immediately on God's creative activity as on its transcendent origin or cause (Transcendental causality).

Applying this theory of 'becoming' to the evolution of man from sub-human forms and eventually from inorganic matter, we may say that man is made not partly by evolutionary forces and partly by God, but wholly by the former and wholly by the latter on a completely different level. God is the transcendent and immediate ground of the whole evolutionary dynamism. The creative relation between God and man is different from the relation between God and brutes or a purely material being precisely because the two creatures are different and different in kind. The creation is 'special' because the thing created is in a class by itself, not because of some special intervention by God in the net of secondary causes. Thus, the creation of man, including his spiritual capacities, should not be regarded in itself as an exceptional, extraordinary or miraculous occurrence but an event which exemplifies in an eminent way all true becoming and self-transcendence. God's creative activity unfolds wherever there is true development and evolution.

Let us ask again the question whether this new account of man's spiritual nature is compatible with the Bible and the official teaching of the Church.

'Soul' in the Bible

In the Old Testament, there are three words that come close to the meaning of 'soul'; *nephesh, rûach* and *n*e*shamah. Nephesh* is a very frequently occurring noun in the Hebrew Bible (over 700 times) indicating 'living being' or some 'vital activity' such as appetite or emotion of a living organism. It is used both for human and animal life. If it is used for humans, *nephesh* corresponds to the 'person' or simply 'what man is' or 'what man has'. In the Hebrew mentality *nephesh* is not understood in contrast to the 'body' or 'flesh'; hence, if it is translated by the word 'soul', it never means a soul distinct from the body. *Nephesh* can be 'dead' (Num 6.6; Lev 21.7), or can mean 'blood' (Deut 12.23f.).

Rûach means 'wind' or 'spirit of God', or 'man's breath' or is simply synonymous with *nephesh. N*e*shamah* is commonly translated as 'breath'. It is either directly coming from God (Gen 2.7; Job 32.8; 33.4; 34.14) or it is a thing that God has made (Is 57.16), or simply means 'man'. The biblical *basar,* which is the closest term in Hebrew for 'body', in its reference to a human being, always indicates the whole man or his activities. The important thing is that in the Old Testament there is no dichotomy between 'soul' and 'body'. Words which come close in their meanings to either of them always indicate the whole animated composite.

In the New Testament *psyche* is the term which corresponds to *nephesh* and is commonly rendered in English as 'soul'. It can mean the living being, the principle of life in a living organism, or life in general. Through Platonic influences it is sometimes thought of in contrast to the body (Mt 10.28), and considered immortal (Apoc 6.9; 20.4) but not always (Mt 20.28; Jn 10.11). It can also refer to animals as in Apoc 16.3: 'and every living thing *(psyche)* died that was in the sea'.

To conclude this brief summary, we may say that the Bible does not regard man as an eternal soul temporarily attached to a mortal body but as a finite creature of flesh, living by the power of God who gives man his whole being as it is. The new account of man's spiritual nature outlined above is not only compatible with the Bible, but, on the whole, it seems to us more in conformity with the Biblical view of man than the old, traditional account.

The earliest formulations of the Church on the soul were not concerned with the soul's immateriality. The Platonic doctrine of a body-soul dichotomy enjoyed a revival in the first century B.C., and had a lasting influence on the Christian notion of the soul. According to this doctrine, the soul belongs to the divine realm; hence it is pre-existent in regard to body, immortal and indestructible. During man's life, the soul is confined to the body as a prisoner to his prison. Subject as he is to change and decay, man's life consists of conflict and struggle. But if someone lives for the divine, eternal realities, at death his soul is released from the prison of his mortal body and returns to the divine realm.

From the point of view of the Christian understanding of man, this Platonic doctrine suggested the following erroneous views:

1. The soul is not created from nothing but it is of the divine substance.
2. The soul is tied to the body as a punishment.
3. The soul has a pre-corporeal existence.
4. Body and matter are evil.
5. Body and soul are not united substantially; man is not one.

The first four of these erroneous views were in fact taught by the Priscillianists, members of a Manichean sect in Spain, founded by Priscillian (died in 385), and condemned by the *Council of Braga* (561) in Portugal.

That in man there are not two souls, one for the sensual, one for the spiritual life, was decreed by the *Council of Constantinople* (869-70) against the supposed teaching of Photius, Patriarch of Constantinople:

Both the Old and the New Testaments teach, and all the enlightened Fathers and Doctors of the Church profess the same opinion, that man has one rational and intellectual soul. Nevertheless... certain people have impudently taught that he has two souls and attempt to justify this heresy with unreasonable arguments...

This Holy General Council therefore anathematises... the inventors of such an impiety (Dz 657-8).

The *Council of Vienne* (1311-12) was also concerned with the unity of man. Its decrees were issued against the errors of *Peter John Olieu* (1248-98), who taught that the soul as a spiritual entity is not directly associated with the material body, but only through a distinct principle, the principle of sensible organic life. The Council safeguarded the unity of man by not allowing any split in man's life into a spiritual and a sensible realm: the soul is the sole principle of man's life.

The Council formulated its teaching with the help of some Aristotelian categories, such as 'form' and 'substance'; but this dependence on a certain philosophical system should not be regarded as essential. Those Aristotelian categories were presupposed and used rather than asserted, and so the dogmatic definition does not entail the acceptance of those categories.

...with the approval of the said Holy Council, we reject as erroneous and contrary to the truth of the Catholic faith any doctrine or position which rashly asserts, or leaves it open to doubt, that the substance of the rational or intellectual soul is not truly and of itself the form of the human body. So that the truth of the pure faith shall be known to all, and that the entry of all errors that might slip in shall be barred, we define that from now on whoever shall presume to assert, defend, or obstinately hold that the rational or intellectual soul is not in itself and essentially the form of the human body, is to be censured as a heretic (Dz 902).

In order to explain the 'descent' of original sin to all men, some Armenians supposedly taught that the human soul was generated by the parents (Traducianism). Pope Benedict XII in 1341 condemned this error, which was formulated in the official document as follows:

> A teacher among the Armenians... taught that the human soul of the son is generated by the body, and that angels also come one from another, for since the human rational soul and the angels, intellectual by nature, are beings like spiritual lights, they generate other spiritual lights from themselves (Dz 1007).

In the sixteenth century, the *Fifth Lateran Council* defined the individuality and the immortality of the human soul (Eighth Session, 1513). The reason for the definition was the defence of faith against the teaching of Pietro Pomponazzi (1464-1525) and that of some others who revived the Averroistic conception of the human soul. According to this, man as an individual somehow has a share in the universal spirit of man while he lives, but, because he is bound up with matter, when he dies the principle of his individual life (his soul) ceases with it. From the definition of the Council is not clear whether the immortality of the individual soul must be regarded as a natural quality of its spirituality or a special gift of God.

> Since the sower of cockle, ancient enemy of the human race... has dared to oversow and to cause to grow in the field of the Lord certain most pernicious errors always rejected by the Faithful, in particular concerning the nature of the rational soul, viz. that it is mortal, or that one and the same soul is found in all men, and since some people, rash in their philosophical thinking, assert this to be, at least philosophically speaking, true; We, therefore, desirous of applying the appropriate remedy to such a mischief, and with the approval of this sacred Council, condemn and reject all those who assert that the intellectual soul is mortal or one soul common to all men, or

who call in doubt that it [the soul] is not only truly and of itself and essentially the form of the human body, as is stated in the canon of Clement V, Our Predecessor of blessed memory, issued by the Council of Vienne, but is also immortal and can be multiplied in accordance with the multitude of bodies into which it is infused, has been and will be so multiplied... (Dz 1440).

Finally, we have the encyclical *Humani Generis* (1950) which teaches: 'that souls are immediately created by God is a view which the Catholic faith imposes on us'. We have already discussed the theological value of this statement in connection with original sin. We have also pointed out that if we accept Rahner's theory of transcendental causality, then this statement of the encyclical must be interpreted in a new light: 'immediate creation of the soul' will no longer be contrasted to the 'mediate creation of the body' through evolution, but it will refer to the particular and distinctive character of the whole man in creation. The whole man is the result of evolution, and still a part of it. As such he is immediately created, just as everything else, but his relation to the Creator is different, and different in kind, from the relation of animals, plants and non-living matter to God. Man is capable of knowing and loving his Creator, and is called by God to a personal fellowship in Christ. 'Though made of body and soul, man is one. Through his bodily composition he gathers to himself the elements of the material world. Thus they reach their crown through him, and through him raise their voice in free praise of the Creator' (*Pastoral Constitution of the Church in the Modern World,* Vatican II, n. 14).

We think that the new interpretation of the creation of the soul is not incompatible with the documents of the Magisterium; on the contrary, when rightly understood, it gives a deeper significance and greater grandeur to their teaching.

CHAPTER 4

THE EVOLUTIONARY VISION OF TEILHARD

In the recent past perhaps no one has done more to help us to see that evolution can be understood in the context of Christian faith than the French Jesuit scientist *Pierre Teilhard de Chardin* (1881-1955). For him evolution was not merely a scientific theory which he had to reconcile cautiously with certain teachings of his Christian faith but a passionate, personal conviction which was so united to his Christian faith that he could see in the manifold, evolving changes of the world God's continuous creative and saving activity. He summed up his vision in the following few sentences:

I believe that the universe is an evolutionary process. I believe that evolution tends in the direction of spirit. I believe that spirit culminates in the personal. I believe that the consummation of the personal is the cosmic Christ (*Comment je crois,* Introduction).

It must be said immediately that certain phrases of Teilhard do not commend him to the British reader. Teilhard was French in spirit, in his style and presentation. Many of his expressions which in their original language have a subtle, poetical and almost mystical character may seem when rendered into English, pretentious, spurious and unintelligible. It must also be realised that much of Teilhard's writing does not qualify either as science or theology. In his bold vision he went much further than what the supporting scientific or theological evidence would strictly allow. Teilhard's achievement was greater than that of a successful professional theologian or scientist. He was a successful myth-maker for the twentieth-century man. Obviously, here we do not use 'myth' in any pejorative sense of the word. We do not equate 'myth' with nonsense, a piece of imagination or simple allegory. Nor do we contrast it simply to an established scientific theory or a historical fact. Authentic myths always intend to express the deepest truths about man and his world in a form which is concrete, vivid and imaginative. Often, they defy commonsense or rational analysis; yet they are not arbitrary creations of the human mind. They build on the contemporary knowledge of the world of man, but are addressed to every man. They have a self-involving character. They open to us new horizons by which we can see ourselves and the world as an ordered whole.

If this description of 'myth' is acceptable, then the use of 'myth' in connection with Teilhard's vision is not unjustified. He certainly built that vision on a vast amount of contemporary scientific knowledge but he extended the concept of evolution in an imaginative way. He related divergent phenomena into a single pattern, into a unifying whole. Through his vision, man's scientific knowledge and his basic Christian beliefs will become somehow organised and explained. His vision suggests a meaning to the world and to man's existence. As such it has an appeal not only to man's intellect but also to his emotions and the whole man. It is indubitable that many, including non-Christians, have been inspired by Teilhard's vision. It deserves serious consideration and cannot be passed by even in a small book like ours. Here we restrict ourselves to a brief exposition of his ideas which were presented to us in his book *The Phenomenon of Man*.

Evolving Universe

The fundamental importance of *The Phenomenon of Man* is that in it the author commits himself unreservedly to an evolutionary pattern of history. Evolution provides the basic framework within which, as he believes, philosophy and theology must henceforth develop. Teilhard claims that his work is a 'phenomenology', i.e. he is not proposing explanations of why things happen as they do, but only a new vision of how they happen. He provides a context for philosophy, rather than a philosophy. In practice, we do not think that he keeps to this programme consistently. Indeed, it would seem to be impossible to describe anything as complicated as the world without making philosophical judgments. But it is important to keep this intention in mind and to attach full weight to it, when criticising the soundness of his work. Essentially, Teilhard is claiming that his conclusions should be judged by their conformity to the observable patterns of the universe as established by modern science, rather than by their agreement with traditional ways of thought which have been coloured more or less deeply and unconsciously by an obsolete world-picture. This claim deserves at least a sympathetic consideration. In the exposition which follows, we shall divide Teilhard's work into two parts, dealing respectively with the pattern of world history up to the appearance of man, and with the present and future pattern of human history. In each case, we shall be less concerned with a detailed exegesis of his text than with an attempt to evaluate the basic ideas upon which it is constructed.

Teilhard distinguishes three main aspects or characteristics of the universe: plurality, unity, energy. We will consider these in turn.

1. *Plurality.* This is a familiar feature of the world which does not require detailed consideration here. Almost everyone would agree that the world does consist in some sense of a number of distinct individual bodies.

2. *Unity.* In its understanding of the unity of the world, modern science goes far beyond the ancient philosophers. Every particle in the universe, we now know, acts upon and is acted upon by every other particle by virtue of its gravitational and, sometimes, by its electro-magnetic forces; per-

haps also in other ways. If the general theory of relativity is accepted, the relation between the individual particle and the universe is even more intimate; every particle helps to determine the fundamental space-time structure of the universe as a whole; one particle more or less would make the whole intrinsic structure of the world slightly different from what it is now. Whether we accept this conclusion or not, it is clear that the highly unified, universally interrelated structure of the modern scientific universe provides a possible ground for world-finality or cosmic pattern, which was not available in the much more loosely inter-connected world of the ancients.

3. *Energy.* This is more or less identical with activity or the power of things to act. The term has a wider and somewhat vaguer connotation than has the energy of the physicist, but there is a general correspondence between the two. It is by virtue of its energy that the universe develops according to a definite, intrinsic, purposive pattern. We must consider now what this pattern is.

For Teilhard, the universe has an intrinsic tendency to evolve, and in doing so, to form progressively more complex structures. It is in process of transition from unorganised plurality to complex unity. Teilhard distinguishes two different sorts of tendency, called respectively radial and tangential energy. Radial energy produces more highly 'centred' (i.e. more organised and unified) structures out of less complex components; tangential energy unifies an aggregate at the same level of organisation as the components themselves.

These ideas can best be illustrated by examples. Suppose we start with a system consisting of two elementary particles, a proton and an electron, moving at random, more or less independently of one another. As they approach each other, their mutual tendencies towards unification or 'complexification' come into play and they combine to form a hydrogen atom. In this, the two particles lose their original

75

independence and exist henceforth in an organised and highly-unified system manifesting a mathematical order which was entirely lacking before the reaction occurred.

Let us suppose now that the hydrogen atom is part of a star in the early stages of its development. Such a star will be almost entirely composed of hydrogen. As its age increases, however, the tendency to 'complexification' will proceed further; hydrogen atoms will combine together to form more complex and more highly ordered helium atoms. Subsequently by successive stages, more and more complex atoms will be formed until, at least in certain stars, under suitable conditions, all the known types of atom will have been produced. Some of the material so formed may be thrown off from the star and, by some process not yet fully understood, may then aggregate into a planet such as the earth. At a certain stage in the earth's history, a new type of aggregate began to be produced: atoms combined with each other to form molecules. The molecule represents a new type of complex, less firmly but more elaborately unified than the atom, having its own characteristic mathematical structure.

The processes so far described have all been manifestations of radial energy, producing more highly organised structures. At this stage, however, as the earth cooled down a new type of ordering appeared, attributed to tangential energy. This is solidification with its usual concomitant of crystallisation. Crystallisation does not involve any increase in organisation or 'centredness'; it is a process by which atoms or molecules spontaneously arrange themselves according to a definite geometrical pattern – a process, therefore, whereby order comes out of disorder but at essentially the same level of organisation as existed previously. Crystallisation is a 'dead-end' so far as evolution is concerned.

However, the radial energy of things is not exhausted; it still continues to operate under suitable circumstances. Besides the tendency to simple crystallisation, there is another at work which, at least under the conditions of the primitive earth, led to the production of larger, more complex and more 'centred' molecules. This occurred particularly among molecules containing two or more of the elements carbon, hydrogen, oxygen and nitrogen. These tended to combine together to form more and more complex molecules, resembling more or less closely the proteins, nucleic acids etc. which form the material basis of living organisms. Eventually a stage was reached at which a molecule or aggregate of molecules acquired a new level or organisation, a new unity and a new range of potentialities, which we call life. Living things have their tangential energy, causing them to multiply by fission or reproduction at the same level of organisation which they themselves manifest, but they also have radial energy which at this stage takes on the familiar form of biological evolution.

Teilhard describes in some detail the main features of the evolutionary process from the original hypothetical organism, up to the much more complex and highly organised types to which they eventually gave rise. One particular line of development he sees, quite rightly, to have a particular significance. This is the line of vertebrate evolution through the primitive fishes, reptiles and mammals to man. In it the process of increasing organisation takes a form which he calls 'cerebralisation' characterised by an increasingly complex central nervous system and brain. It is only by this means, and only when the system has reached a suitable degree of elaboration, that biological evolution can reach its crown and fulfilment in man.

Aspects of 'Within' and 'Without'

At every level at which matter can exist Teilhard sees in it two really distinct but essentially linked aspects which he calls the 'within' and the 'without' – 'inside' and 'outside'.

The without is that aspect with which physical science is primarily concerned – its description in terms of space and time. The within is the aspect which, in the case of living things, would be the province of the psychologist. Thus, in the case of a free human action, the without would be described in terms of the structure and activities of the nervous system, muscles etc., resulting in a series of movements of the limbs; the within would require a different set of categories such as desires, intentions, choices. In the case of an animal or human act involving sensation, the without would consist in descriptions of the nervous system, of the sense organs and their physical reaction to suitable stimuli; the within would be concerned with sensations as experienced by the organism, with the intrinsic qualities of colour, sound, pain, taste etc. To say that we see the blue of the sky is not to say that our sense organs are being stimulated in a particular way by light or a particular wavelength; nevertheless the two types of description cannot be dissociated; they refer to one and the same situation seen from two different points of view, really distinct but not physically separable. It is one of Teilhard's fundamental principles that this duality of aspect – the within and without or, in a rather broad sense, the psychic and the physical – is to be found not only in living things but at all levels of being. If we wish to describe the path of the earth round the sun from without we should state a mathematical formula for its path; to describe it from within we should say that a body left to itself has a tendency to travel in a straight line at uniform velocity, that any two bodies have a tendency to attract one another, and that the actual movement of the earth is the resultant of these two tendencies. The path of a body in space and time belongs to the outer description, its tendencies (which are in some sense goal-seeking) to the inner. Similarly, a magnetic compass could be described either in mathematical terms – its geometrical orientation and its mode of oscillation – or we could say that it 'seeks' to orientate itself in a particular direction relative to the earth. Both descriptions are valid, but they describe different aspects of the same situation. Both are, in fact, commonly used; even the physicist talks about the 'north-seeking' pole of a magnet.

Teilhard maintains that there is a real continuity of meaning between, say, an animal seeking food and a magnet seeking the north; between a male and female uniting in the act of generation and two atoms uniting to form a chemical compound. This is not to say, of course, that the meaning is precisely the same in each case, but it does imply that there is more than a mere figure of speech when we apply terms such as seeking or tending to inorganic things. Atoms are not alive, but we can apply to them a category of 'pre-life' which can be regarded as a very rudimentary and undifferentiated form of consciousness and even of sensitivity. The process of evolution implies, not the sudden appearance out of nothing, of life, consciousness and sensitivity, but rather an elaboration, organisation, 'centring', of a quality which was there inchoately from the beginning.

The Appearance of Man

As we have remarked before, according to Teilhard, among the various lines of biological evolution the most significant is the line of vertebrate evolution through the primitive fishes, amphibians and reptiles to the mammals. In its outer aspect the characteristic feature of this line of development is the steadily increasing complexity of the brain and central nervous system, by virtue of which the various parts of the organism become more differentiated and at the same time more precisely co-ordinated, thus producing the possibility of a progressively greater range of activity adapted to different circumstances. The inner aspect of the process is manifested as an increasing complexity and centredness of

79

psychic life represented, on the one hand, by increasing capacities for perceiving, remembering and learning by experience, and on the other by an increasing capacity to unify and organise experience.

The final stage of the evolutionary process is the appearance of man. The transition from ape to man represents, in its outer or physical aspect, a relatively small change, the most important feature of which is an increase in size and complexity of the brain. The corresponding change in the psychic order – the inner aspect – is, however, of very profound importance. Man becomes capable not only of having experiences but of reflecting on them. He becomes self-conscious. The process of unification thus becomes, in a sense, complete. A new level of life and consciousness has been reached.

Teilhard is, we think, right in seeing in man's power of reflection the most characteristic expression of his essential difference from all other physical things. A being who can reflect on himself and his world is no longer wholly subject to matter and to the laws of the physical world. In one aspect of his personality he is above the limitations of a material being. He can judge the world, its laws and its limitations, and his judgment is not simply a product of physical law, but proceeds from a supra-material spiritual principle. Only a free, rational, spiritual being can be aware of the causes and motives which guide him, and can reflect on his own acts and judgments.

Spiritual and Social Evolution

It is of the essence of Teilhard's theory that the pattern of history is not yet complete. The world is still in process of moving towards its final goal or consummation. Up to the present, there have been two main stages: first the production of progressively larger molecules by physico-chemical processes, and secondly the process of biological evolution. The first of these was ordered towards the production of a living organism and had no further evolutionary significance once this point has been reached; the second was ordered to the production of more and more complex and psychically centred organisms and has been essentially completed with the appearance of man. It is unlikely that the human race will evolve much further in the physical order, though minor improvements will not presumably be excluded. This does not mean, however, that the cosmic process has now come to a stop. It will continue but in future it will be concerned with man's spiritual development and, in particular, with his relations to other men in society. The line of evolution will be social rather than individual.

In order to understand Teilhard's ideas on this question it will be necessary to consider briefly the general nature of man's relation to the society of which he is a member. There are two extreme views on the subject: individualism and collectivism. Individualism regards the individual as the absolute entity. Each human being exists primarily for his own self-perfection. Society exists in order to provide him with a suitable environment for the purpose and to ensure that different individuals do not unduly obstruct each other in their respective efforts at self-realisation. We should work for others (in moderation), partly because unselfishness is virtuous and the practice of virtue perfects ourselves; partly because we hope that others will be unselfish in our regard. But always the ultimate motive of our actions should be our own good. Collectivism, on the other hand, regards society as the absolute entity; the individual exists simply as a means to promote the good of society and has no absolute value in himself.

Neither of these theories, if pushed to extremes, can produce a healthy social order. The one tends to make of society a mere instrument for the protection of the rights and privileges of the strong as against the weak; the other diminishes the dignity of the human person and in so doing corrupts the society of which he is a member. Neither has within itself the potentiality for indefinite growth in perfection. Sooner or later they will degenerate or collapse, to be replaced by some other type. In practice, existing societies tend to be an uneasy compromise, in which the conflict of interest between individual and collectivity is mitigated as far as possible, but never solved.

Omega Point

On Teilhard's theory it is possible to steer a course between the Scylla of individualism and the Charybdis of collectivism, not by compromising but by genuinely transcending them. We can conceive of a human society whose members, without any sacrifice of their own dignity and perfection, are so perfectly united in mind and heart that they have, in effect, a single intellect and will and have become a 'hyperperson'. It is towards this end that the pattern of history is now orientated. This is the direction in which evolution must and will henceforth proceed. The final goal is called the Omega point and is, in some sense which is not made altogether explicit, to be identified with God.

This theory raises a number of problems which can be classified under four main heads:

(1) Can we envisage a process of hyper-personalisation which preserves intact (or enhances) the dignity and intrinsic value of the individual?

(2) Does the theory leave room for the distinction between the natural and supernatural elements in human history, which is fundamental to Catholic theology?

(3) Is the postulate of a steady and, in a sense, preordained evolution to a state of perfection on this earth compatible with the doctrine of original sin?

(4) Is the distinction between God and the ultimate ter-

restrial society on the one hand, and between the Mystical Body of Christ and the ultimate terrestrial society on the other, sufficiently safeguarded?

We will briefly consider these in order.

Interrelation between Individual and Society

In some sense it seems clear that a society is more than the mere sum of its members and to this extent can be regarded as a hyper-personal entity. When two human beings meet and converse as social beings they cease to be isolated and independent individuals, like two beans which happen to be next to one another in a sack. The communication of mind with mind brings into being new types of perfection which could not in principle be realised in a single individual. Mutual understanding, sympathy, love are essentially products of social life. They are emergent qualities which can only exist in a society, yet without them a man cannot be truly human. A human being who was brought up from infancy without any contact with other people would never be able to realise his specifically human potentialities. A child learns to think, to speak, to love, to behave morally, only by intercourse with other persons. Apart from some special divine intervention there is no other way in which he can acquire these abilities, without which he could not live a human life. Man is intrinsically dependent on society. To a large extent, though not in a strictly deterministic sense, it moulds his character and makes him a man. It is legitimate, therefore, to look upon a human society as something more than its members. It realises new perfections which could not exist in a single individual; it has, in a sense, a unity of its own and a life of its own. Although the analogy must not be pressed too far, it can be compared to a living organism of which the individual persons are the particular organs. An organ is essentially ordered to the body of which it is a member, and can only realise its potentialities within the body. The same is true analogously of the relation of man to society.

The minimum society in which a human being would be able to develop as such could consist, in principle, of two persons only, but this would be too small for anything like complete self-realisation. There is a love of man and wife, of parent and child, of brother and sister; friendships based on similarity of temperament or contrast of temperament; affection arising from sympathy, admiration, gratitude. Our intellectual life may be enriched by intercourse with persons of the most diverse interests and abilities; our emotional life by an innumerable variety of artistic achievements. All these make possible a fuller realisation of human nature. The larger and more diversified the society, the greater will be the scope for actualising the capacities of human nature for knowledge and love. In practice the possibilities are limited by the fact that, as a society increases in size, the bond of unity becomes weaker, conflicts of interest arise, mutual understanding becomes more difficult. Society in practice generates misunderstanding as well as understanding, discord as well as harmony, hate as well as love. The result is likely to be war, internal disintegration, or the imposition of a forced and artificial unity by the suppression of legitimate realisations of the human spirit. This, however, is an accidental limitation even though its source is deeply rooted in human nature. There is no reason in principle why the whole human race should not constitute one society in which each member achieves the highest possible self-realisation in complete harmony and concord with every other. In such a society it could be said that in a real and important sense there was 'one heart and one soul'. From it the individual would, under God, receive the possibility of living a full human life; to it he would make his own essential contribution. It would be a true hyper-personal unity, yet the persons who constituted it would lose nothing of dignity or perfection by being incorporated into it. It is towards a unity of this sort that the human race, according to Teilhard, is now moving, although it must be clearly understood that the ultimate society will not be a purely human one, but will have God as its centre and principle of unity.

How long this process will take for completion we cannot even guess. But there are clear indications that an important step forward is being taken at the present time. Up till now, the human race has been divided into a number of distinct, more or less isolated and self-sufficient societies. With the present increase in world population this will no longer be possible. The threat of over-population has made it impossible to maintain the old exclusiveness and has made the real interests of all humanity the same. We are living in one world and it is inevitable that we shall have to constitute one society. It is as if a number of fragmentary crystals were being put into the melting-pot to be fused together. It may be long and laborious before a single perfect crystal emerges from the melt, but the present breaking up of the old and exclusive boundaries is an essential step forward.

The ultimate hyper-personal society is called by Teilhard the Omega point and it is identified, in some sense, with God. Teilhard has on this account sometimes been accused of pantheistic tendencies but it is clear that this was not his intention. The Omega point represents a 'theanthropic' unity – a union of humanity with God in which God is the ultimate principle of unity – but God is not identical with humanity. He remains transcendent. The Omega point, as we shall see later, is in fact the physical realisation or perfection of the Mystical Body of Christ.

A Single Pattern of Creation and Salvation

The movement of humanity towards the hyper-personal Omega point belongs, according to Teilhard, to the same pattern of history as the process of complexification in the inorganic and biological realms. From first to last it is a manifestation of the radial energy of the world producing unity in complexity, and in doing so opening up new possibilities of richer and more integrated life and consciousness. It is because a single pattern can be discerned throughout that we can confidently predict the broad outline of future development. At this point, however, certain theological difficulties arise. Christian theology recognises in world-history one critical point to which all that went before is related, to which all that comes after looks back: the moment of the Incarnation of the Son of God. By virtue of the Incarnation the order of creation, in which the world was constituted before the coming of man, has been superseded by the order of grace. Man finds himself called to a destiny which far exceeds any goal which a created being could possibly attain by his own powers. Hence we should expect to find two different patterns in world-history, applying respectively to the periods before and after the appearance of man, with a definite discontinuity between the two. Teilhard certainly recognises the distinction between the order of creation and the order of grace, but it does not play the fundamental role in his view of history which might be expected. Essentially, for him, there is still one underlying pattern.

There are two considerations which explain and, we think, justify Teilhard's position on this point. In the first place, he holds that the tendency to hyper-personal unity is inherent in the creation of man. Basically, therefore, it is a natural phenomenon; it belongs to him by virtue of his participation in the created order of things. But it is not ultimately bound to, or limited by, this order. God can take an existing natural tendency and raise it to a higher level undreamed of by merely natural reason. And he can do this by a transformation which involves no obvious discontinuity in the course of history. Grace perfects nature, and does not simply replace it. Indeed, from the very beginning God destined man to share in the gifts which were in fact brought by the divine condescension of the Incarnation: the world was created with this end in view. The whole of creation is, and was from the first moment, oriented towards that participation in the divine nature which Christ brings to the human race. In the actual order the movement towards hyper-personality was planned to have its final consummation in the Mystical Body of Christ. It was for this purpose that God gave atoms the tendency to aggregate into molecules, molecules to form living cells, living cells to move along the line of evolution which culminates in man, man to unite with his fellows in a society whose ultimate goal and purpose should be a union patterned upon the hyper-personal unity of the Blessed Trinity and culminating in the Beatific Vision.

Original Sin in the Teilhardian Scheme

Traditional theologians have always attached great importance to the doctrine of Original Sin. In Teilhard's system, on the other hand, it has a less dominant position. He took the view that in an evolving universe where humanity, by the nature of the case, is engaged in a process of development from a less perfect to a more perfect state – from ignorance, weakness and inexperience to knowledge, strength and experience – we must expect that there will be frequent failure, frustration and evil. In principle, no special or extraordinary explanation of this phenomenon need be looked for. Teilhard recognised, however, that the actual extent and intensity of evil in this world may be more than can be reasonably accounted for by the mere fact that man is situated in an evolving world. He was therefore willing to concede that the problem may have been exacerbated by some more specific moral dislocation at the beginning of human history. But this question never occupied a prominent position in his thought.

Many critics have objected that he has here been unfaithful to the orthodox Christian position. However, as we have already seen in Chapter 3, there is a fairly widespread tendency among contemporary theologians to move away from the older theories of the Fall and Original Sin, and to reinterpret the doctrine in a way which comes much closer to Teilhard's position. While it may be doubted whether his idea of evolving humanity could ever be reconciled with the extreme view of Adam as the perfect archetype of man, it is quite consistent with the idea that some special principle of evil has invaded human history and has made man's progress more painful and problematic than it need have been.

The Historical Realisation of the Mystical Body of Christ

Teilhard recognises that even at the end, when the final unity is attained, there may be some part of the human race which will turn away and refuse to participate. But the tendency to unity is so deeply engrained in human nature and so inextricably woven into the pattern of world-history from the beginning that we cannot suppose that it will be finally frustrated.

This is not an unreasonable expectation. Man's nature is disordered, but it is not beyond all healing. Christ has restored contact between man and God. By virtue of the sacramental system, even the purely material world participates in the process of reuniting all things to God. The Church, as the visible body of Christ, is ceaselessly at work sanctifying the world, and there is no reason, in the nature of things, why the effect should not be a progressive drawing of the whole human race nearer to God. We do not think we can know for certain that this will be the case, and Teilhard is perhaps over-optimistic in suggesting that we can. It is conceivable that all the graces channelled on to this earth through the sacraments and prayers of the Church will only suffice to hold the forces of evil precariously at bay without securing any permanent advance. To us, engaged in the struggle a mere two thousand years after the foundation of Christianity, it may appear problematical whether there has been much ground gained yet. But on a long-term view it is not unreasonable to hope that there will be a progressive sanctification of the human race and, in a sense, of the whole physical world. That this was one of the purposes of the Incarnation seems to be clearly implied by St Paul when he writes:

> I consider that the sufferings of this present time are not worth comparing with the glory that is to be revealed to us. For the creation waits with eager long-ing for the revealing of the sons of God; for the crea-tion was subjected to futility, not of its own will but by the will of him who subjected it in hope; because the creation itself will be set free from its bondage to decay and obtain the glorious liberty of the children of God. We know that the whole creation has been groaning in travail together until now; and not only the creation, but ourselves who have the first fruits of the Spirit, groan inwardly as we wait for adoption as sons, the redemption of our bodies. For in this hope we were saved. Now hope that is seen is not hope. For who hopes for what he sees? But if we hope for what we do not see, we wait for it with patience (Rom 8.18-25).

Original Sin, however it is to be understood, will always be with us; children will always come into this world de-prived of sanctifying grace and in need of redemption. But it remains possible that the secondary effects of original sin may diminish as the work of restoring all things in Christ proceeds, and the result will be a progressive actualisation of the unity of the mystical Christ on this earth.

This is all the more to be hoped for and expected when we consider that there is no other way, before the day of the Last Judgement, in which the Mystical Body can be realised in its fullness. Catholic eschatology, since the Middle Ages, has tended perhaps to concentrate too much on individual salvation and to see the history of redemption simply as a sequence of individual souls reaching their rewards one by one and then, at the Last Day, receiving their body as a personal increment to their glory. For Teilhard, on the other hand, the focal point of interest is the gradual and progressive restoration of the whole physical creation to Christ, and with it the gradual development of a mystical union of human persons (not merely human souls) in the Body of Christ. When that Body has been perfected, the souls who have gone before, and whose merits and prayers will have contributed so much in its realisation, will take their allotted place in it as persons.

> After that will come the end, when he [Christ] hands over the kingdom to God the Father, having done away with every sovereignty, authority and power. For he must be King until he has put all his enemies under his feet and the last of his enemies to be destroyed is death... And when everything is subjected to him, then the Son himself will be subject in his turn to the One who subjected all things to him, so that God may be all in all (1 Cor 15.24-28, Jerusalem Bible).

If the interpretation of Teilhard's views which has been proposed in these pages is correct, there does not seem to be anything unorthodox in them. Teilhard's vision suggests a new way of approaching the traditional problems of Catholic theology and philosophy and a new synthesis of these with the modern scientific world-picture, but it does not undermine any basic theological doctrine. Teilhard's synthesis has its defects: its terminology is often obscure and unsatisfactory; it tends to overemphasise certain aspects of the picture and to ignore others; the final conclusions are given an air of inevitability which may not be justified. But when all legitimate criticism has been made, it seems to us that Teilhard's vision of the universe as a unity in which all things are orientated towards the final consummation in the Mystical Body of Christ, is both reasonable and important. His ideas should be a stimulus and inspiration to theologians for many years to come.

SELECT BIBLIOGRAPHY

General

I. G. Barbour: *Issues in Science and Religion* (Prentice Hall, 1966)

A. Hulsbosch: *God's Creation* (Sheed & Ward, 1965, p.b.)

E. C. Messenger: *Evolution and Theology* (Burns Oates, 1951)

K. Rahner: *Hominisation* (Burns & Oates, 1965, p.b.)

P. Schoonenberg: *God's World in the Making* (Duquesne University Press, 1961)

Concilium vol. 6, no. 3 (June 1967). This number of the journal is devoted to the problems of evolution.

Chapter 1

C. Darwin: *The Origin of Species* (John Murray, 6th edition, 1886)

C. Darwin: *The Descent of Man* (John Murray, 2nd edition, 1894)

T. Dobzhansky: *Mankind Evolving* (Yale University Press, 1962)

J. Huxley: *Evolution, the Modern Synthesis* (George Allen & Unwin, 1942)

P. Teilhard de Chardin: *The Vision of the Past* (Collins, 1966)

Chapter 2

Z. Alszeghi: 'Development in the Doctrinal Formulations of the Church concerning the Theory of Evolution' in *Concilium*, vol. 6, no. 3, p. 14f.

W. Bröker: 'Aspects of Evolution' in *Concilium*, op. cit., p. 5f.

A. Ellegård: *Darwin and the General Reader* (Göteborg University Press, 1958)

See also the books of Rahner, Hulsbosch and Schoonenberg listed under the General Bibliography.

Chapter 3

V. Baumann: *Erbsünde?* (Herder, 1970)

A. M. Dubarle: *The Biblical Doctrine of Original Sin* (Geoffrey Chapman, 1964)

J. De Fraine: *Adam and the Family of Man* (Alba House, 1966)

R. North: *Teilhard and the Creation of the Soul* (Bruce, 1966)

K. Rahner: 'Evolution and Original Sin' (in *Concilium* vol. 6 no. 2, June 1967, p 30f.)

J. A. T. Robinson: *The Body* (SCM Press, 1952)

E. J. Yarnold: *The Theology of Original Sin* (Mercier Press, 1972)

Chapter 4

P. Teilhard de Chardin: *The Phenomenon of Man* (Collins, 1959, p.b.)

P. Teilhard de Chardin: *Man's Place in Nature* (Collins, 1966)

P. Teilhard de Chardin: *Le Milieu Divin* (Fontana, 1964, p. b.)

H. de Lubac: *The Religion of Teilhard de Chardin* (Collins, 1967)

C. F. Mooney: *Teilhard de Chardin and the Mystery of Christ* (Collins, 1966)

P. Smulders: *La vision de Teilhard de Chardin* (Desclée de Brouwer, 1964)

M. N. Wildiers: *An Introduction to Teilhard de Chardin* (Fontana, 1968, p.b.)

INDEX

October, 1972.

    26   The Theology of Confirmation by Austin P. Milner, O.P.

    37   The Theology of Mission by Aylward Shorter, W.F.

November, 1972.

    13   The Theology of God by Andrew Lascaris, O.P.

    36   The Theology of Angels and Devils by Rob van der Hart, O.P.

February, 1973.

    15   Why were the Gospels Written? by John Ashton, S.J.

    33   The Priest as Preacher by Edward P. Echlin, S.J.

March, 1973.

    27   Theology of the Eucharist by James Quinn, S.J.

    43   The Church and the World by Rodger Charles, S.J.

    44   Roman Catholicism, Christianity and Anonymous Christianity by J. P. Kenny, S.J.